STRINGER'S DASH

EVERY LIFE HAS VALUE AND A LEGACY
TO PASS FORWARD.

FRED STRINGER

FOREWORD BY GARY L. FROST

Beautiful Minds
Publishing

ISBN: 978-1-955228-13-8
Printed in the United States of America

DEDICATION

This book is dedicated to all the hard working, fun loving, serious, silly, family oriented, sometimes up, sometimes down people in this world that represents society's definition of average. Guess what? We also represent most people.

One of the benefits of the "average" status is we get to interact with more people we relate to, people that are in the same or similar boat trying to navigate the circumstances of daily living, and there could be more interaction with people knocking on our doors for a variety of reasons.

This dedication is born and shaped in the hope that when and if a knock comes to our door, we will open it with the understanding that this has the possibility of becoming a transitional period in someone's life. Perhaps an opportunity to help mentor someone through a difficult period, or simply to come along to celebrate a success or breakthrough.

It could be a knock from someone needing to be encouraged to take the next steps facing the reality of their circumstance, a knock from a friend needing to be uplifted, or a knock from a stranger just needing to talk to someone and they find you.

The answered knocks can be unlimited and shapeless because it will depend on our compassion and ability to recognize the opportunity. It could be as simple as helping to make someone's day or literally as serious as changing someone's life.

The longer we traverse through time living our lives, the more we should understand the uncertainty of tomorrow and respect the notion that things good and bad don't always happen to other people, sometimes they happen to us.

Once you grasp that reality, it's easy to understand that we are all one step or a single incident away from possibly being the one on the other side of the door knocking.

That knock on the door is figuratively speaking, although it could be the knock on an actual door, but more than likely it will be on someone's heart door. That door can be as cold and hard as ice or compassionate and welcoming as a warm summer breeze.

The reason I chose to dedicate my book to people was an easy choice for me. The foundation lies within my prayers and hopes that we as human beings become more compassionate toward other's needs and develop hearts wanting to reach out and make a difference in helping to shape this world into a better place for all of us to cohabitate.

THANK YOU

Writing this book was an adventurous, never attempted before undertaking for me. Over time I sought feedback on my overall writing style and subject content by letting people of diverse backgrounds, ethnicities, and demographics read some early chapters for honest feedback. There were others that provided research, encouragement, and professional direction at times. This is my grateful attempt to recognize these individuals and to say, "Thank You" for their efforts.

Ed Robinson

James Herod

Jamie Carpenter

Bob Carson

Pastor Kenneth Donaldson

Dina Hardiman

Pat Powell

Anthony and Sandra Stringer

Gregory Elliot

Joe and Gwen Saunders

Tabitha Patrone

Henry Brown

The LaCivita Family

James Burnette

Brenda Austin

Keith Stringer

Pastor Joe Cameneti

Allan Thompson

Charles Kershaw

Jennifer Stringer

Tarick Bernat

Kimberly Lumpkin

Ernie Brown

Robert and Arbor Hughes

Elsie Rhodes

Mike Owens

Brittany Kershaw

Tim Seman

ACKNOWLEDGMENTS

This book tracks many of the steps I've taken, decisions I've made, and opinions I have on matters and issues of living life. To that end, I feel the need to give special thanks to some key individuals in my life that helped me take that journey, people that poured love into me, trust, discipline, and so much more that has shaped the character of the man who has become Fred Stringer.

Mother and Grandmother, "Little Ma"

For truly forming my early bedrock foundation, for living and seeding confidence in me. Their guidance was grounded in love, and it was a constant reminder of how special they thought I was. I never wanted to disappoint them. They were more precious to me than I'm sure I was ever able to convey.

Father

For always painting a picture of what hard work looked like. A lot of his adult life and all his senior living was spent adjusting away from his life's plan "A." As I watched his story unfold, it reassured me that life still has value when some of your plans don't work out; he never gave up. He taught me humility. I miss our Sunday evening chats on the phone and I'm grateful to be my father's son.

Sandra Lynn Henderson

For saying, "Yes" to becoming my first wife. She was my first love and blessed our family with two wonderful children. She was also a super mom. Even though our time together was a short 22 years, she made every day something I looked forward to sharing with her. I can't count the times she made me feel like I could "leap tall buildings in a single bound!" I miss her still.

Kevin and Nicole

For being two of the highlights of my life and a constant source of pride and love. I have paperwork that states that I'm your father, but I want to say, "thank you" for the pleasure of being your DAD. I'm so proud of the adults and parents you both have grown to become.

Renee' Johnson

For becoming my second wife of now 28 years and counting. We first met at one of the lowest periods in my life. Your love and our relationship elevated me to a place where I could once again feel the light and warmth of the sunny side of life. Our love continues to grow and I'm so very blessed to have you and your family in my life.

Keena, niece

For representing a pillar of courage and faith to all. Whenever I think that I'm having a difficult day, I think of you and the "Pity Party" is over. Hang in there kid, much love!

Loving family and close friends

For helping form the components of who I am today. You mean everything to me!

Jimmy Tiggett

For being my best friend for over 40 years, everybody needs one and mine is exceptional. You're a confidant that I trust completely, and I know you will always have my back. I've always admired the value you place on being a father and the love and leadership you show to your entire family. I tried to get him to adopt me a couple of times, but it didn't work. Love always.

Gary L. Frost

For inviting me to be a part of your family, for being a spiritual mentor to me, and making me want to learn more and more about the word of God. For being my brother and friend for life, for being so generous with your words in the foreword of my book, you were always my plan "A" for that job! You know how I feel about you.

A collective "**Special Thanks**" to all for forming the border pieces to my life's puzzle and to my Lord and Savior Jesus Christ for always securing my four corners.

CONTENTS

FOREWORD by Gary L. Frost

It has been suggested that there's at least one book buried in the bosom of each one of us and the vast majority of those books will unfortunately go unwritten. We all have a story to tell, for some it may be a brief brochure while for others a multi-chaptered masterpiece, but there's a message encrypted in every human being. Thank God, Fred Stringer has set his message free, to his relief and to our benefit.

As I made my way through this bold book, I felt privileged that this man was allowing me as a reader to peak behind his public persona to see the private and personal mechanisms that make him tick. Fred had a lot to risk in being so very transparent; however, such vulnerability serves to reinforce his compelling purpose for writing Stringer's Dash; that generations to come might benefit from his failures as well as his successes. He sees himself as a runner in a relay race committed to doing his best, exchanging the baton, and cheering the next runner on. (See chapter One)

This book is written with a certain air of confidence. I have discovered that all too often a person's confidence can be misinterpreted as their arrogance. Jesus Christ Himself suffered that criticism. Though He was "God made flesh" and therefore the Ultimate Man, He demonstrated the ultimate humility in submitting Himself to the ultimate humiliation of death on a cross. His critics thought he was proud of Himself but in reality, He was passionate for others. Well, Fred is no Messiah, but he has learned from his Savior how to live out his life in humble confidence. Stringer's Dash is written not to glorify Stringer but to provide helpful instruction for those who will dash behind him.

I imagine there are readers who will be a bit offended by Fred's frank and sometimes blunt assessment of the dynamic realities of his African American heritage. For those folks, let me warn you; the purpose of this book is not to soothe and to comfort but rather to disturb and to provoke. It will be obvious as you journey through these pages that Fred's tough love for his family and for his people drives his obligation to "call it as he sees it" and "tell it as he did it." We know that real change can only come through discomfort as someone wisely stated, "You won't change until the pain of staying the same becomes greater than the pain of change."

Fred Stringer is my friend and my brother, and as a leader in the congregation I pastored he was also a colleague. I have learned the danger of surrounding myself with "yes men" who will always agree and never challenge your ideas and your vision. Unfortunately, such people will applaud and smile as you head for the cliff, Fred is surely not a member of that tribe. I could always trust that Fred would "speak the truth in love" and though his perspective might conflict with mine, I could trust that his perspective was genuine and purposed for my betterment and for the mission's success. I love this guy, and he has been an asset in my life and ministry.

Part of the beauty and uniqueness of this book is its inspirational messages that will appeal to people of all backgrounds. I heartily commend this work to you.

So, put on your running shoes and get ready to take the dash. You're in for an exhilarating journey with one of the finest and most authentic men I know.

INTRODUCTION

It's late afternoon on Monday, October 10, 1966, and I'm headed outside for the first 30-minute break of today's training session. I remember being in an upbeat mood because I was saying to myself, "I'll be finished with this eight-week course tomorrow, process out Wednesday, and be at Duluth Air Base in Minnesota for my first assignment/tour on Thursday."

I was excited about the challenge of starting my new job with the skills I had just learned but mostly about changing my location. I was also thinking, "When I leave this f.....-up state, I don't even want to fly over it." My technical training was at Keesler Air Base in Biloxi, Mississippi. This base was riddled with bad experiences and memories in the short time I spent there.

As I'm leaving the building to join the others in class, I hear someone call out, "Airman Stringer, can I have a minute of your time?" It was a familiar voice.

I turn around and see it's one of our instructors, one I had labeled a "good guy." I responded, "Yeah, of course."

The conversation started with him reminding me that the class was ending the next day, and that he had some questions and comments he wanted to share with me. Little did I know the encounter and parts of our conversation would stay with me for a lifetime. The part that has followed me like a shadow was the second question he posed.

His first statement changed the mood I was in. He said, "The day before class started, we the instructors received a message to keep an eye on Stringer. He could be trouble."

All the instructors were White, which gave me pause in the beginning because of the things I had encountered prior to the start of class. However, the classroom setting provided a better atmosphere, and my tensions quickly faded. That message was from the Lieutenant responsible for my housing. He went on to say that they had me on their radar during the classroom activities and they were also observing how I interacted with others during the break periods outside.

Then he asked the first question, "Why did the Lieutenant have that opinion of you?"

My initial response was, "Because he's a sorry-ass-piece-of-shit of a human being." After getting that off my chest, I calmed down and began to explain what happened between us. I talk in detail about that in the chapter "**Growing up in the USAF.**" It was parts of the conversation that followed that had an impact on me.

I shared some of the things I had been through and the ways I had been treated since I had been on the base. The instructor actually apologized for what I experienced and applauded what I had done to address it. He then understood why the Lieutenant had flagged me the way he did.

He stated that he wanted to talk to me because he and the other instructors saw no reason for the warning over the past eight weeks. He expressed that they found me to be hard working, engaging, smart, and unique in a good way. I was told I stood out in the classroom and during the break periods while interacting with various people. He continued that I seemingly was not drawn to the crowd, but the crowd was drawn to me. He also added that I seemed to be perfectly content when I was by myself.

Then came the second question. This question was even more personal, the one with legs and staying power. "What is it about you that so many people seem to be drawn to?"

I was caught so off guard that I just smiled, shrugged my shoulders, and simply said, "I don't know." He smiled back and said he thought I would do very well if I decided to make the military my career, or for that matter any direction life might take me. I thanked him for what he had shared. We shook hands and the conversation was over. The next night at the end of the class, we wished each other good luck and went our separate ways.

Back to the question, what he was really asking was "Who is Fred Stringer and what makes me different?" The truth is, it's a question we all need to probe about ourselves. The question itself is very dynamic and sometimes elusive because parts of the answers evolve over time; we simply can't be described or identified as just one thing.

I believe the real challenge to that question is determining who we are at our core. Once that has been established, understood, and accepted, we begin to understand our movements toward the things we accept and/or reject as each day/situation presents itself.

We struggle with the "core" question because sometimes when other people see things in us and try to push us in one direction or another, for a variety of reasons, we tend to question and sometimes devalue ourselves. When we devalue ourselves, we can get stuck in a maze of "what if" questions that can keep us from moving forward. It's like a type of procrastination but different. It's more like a cause of procrastination because we are questioning whether we can make this "whatever thing" happen.

Do we really not see what others see or do we just not want to move away from our comfort zones? That comfort zone question calls for serious consideration because of the varying ways it can impact a life. On the one hand, it can hold you back from possible opportunities missed, on the other hand it speaks to how you see yourself and that has great value; here's why.

It takes a process over time for most people to get mentally comfortable as to who they are and why. However, most people who get to that level are not easily swayed by situations or other people to change who they are at their core. That means (and this is important) they define themselves and don't let situations or circumstances or people define them. That allows a person to stop riding the guessing game, the "who am I" emotional rollercoaster, and that's a major life accomplishment.

On the other side of that, when people struggle with not letting things define them and parts of who they are don't line up with that image, it could become problematic. If they continue to hide those parts of themselves, their mental health could suffer. After I began to understand some of those dynamics, I started to recognize people that were trapped within that condition.

For most of my adult life I've been told things like, "You missed your calling; you can be a wedding counselor, a motivational speaker. I always learn something, I feel motivated, my spirit is lifted when I'm around you, and so many other complementary things. After many years of doing an autopsy on those comments, I believe I've discovered most of their origins and why people see me the way they do.

One of the things I've learned about life is there are things we do and ways we act that get ingrained in our DNA. Things that we not only get comfortable with but also get very good at; we just don't put labels on them.

One of those for me is getting people to open up to me in conversation, I always knew this was a gift of mine, but I didn't quite know what to call it, now I can put a label on it. I was once part of an eight-week discipleship course at my church that totaled sixteen men. Each week, two of us were given fifteen minutes to share three specific things in three different categories about ourselves.

Most of the presentations, at some point, got very emotional. There were tears shed and things revealed that had been suppressed for years. Taking part in that helped me to understand why people open up to me. I use various methods to give people a safe zone to communicate openly and freely. In that class of all men, the Pastor created a safe zone, and we all felt it.

Another thing I generally do within conversations is play devil's advocate. I will challenge people to see how strongly they can defend the points they are trying to make. I try to get them to consider other options even if I agree with them. People talk and act like they think, but looking at different talking points, you can possibly change how they feel about certain issues. In most cases, there are learning opportunities on both sides.

I believe a big part of the answer to the question, "Why people are drawn to me?" Simply, it's my approach to life and how I treat people.

Imagine a picture puzzle of the issues of life. Like all puzzles, each piece is cut to fit in its specific place. If you try to force a piece into a space where it doesn't belong, it's a problem and the picture gets distorted. What I try to do is help people find the right space/answer to keep their life issues from being distorted and most of them appreciate my efforts.

I believe that how I see life is somewhat unique as compared to the average person. I say that because of some of my experiences, my conversations, and interactions with others, and frankly the attention I've paid over the years to what works and what is problematic.

Part of my learning process was understanding the interactions and workings of the things that have major impacts on our lives that can be positive or negative. Things like how knowledge increases power and control. Things like how experience and relationships impact emotions. Those six components are the driving forces as to how a person lives their life. I say that because they are the major influences that impact our decision making. Our decisions ultimately make up about 80% as to how we will live our lives.

As humans, there is one thing I can say with certainty that we all have in common, we were all born. From there, our lives can take off in endless possible directions because each of us is different in so many ways.

As we travel down our life paths, we at some point begin to drift towards some common ground again by way of some questions we each need to answer. Who are we? What does happiness look and feel like? What does success mean and what is the plan to get there?

There's a very appropriate saying that deals with life experiences, it goes something like this, "I wish that I had known when I was (*fill in the blank*) what I know now, my life could have been a lot different." For the most part, the difference being the decisions made at certain times and situations in our lives.

I've always been in pursuit of better ways of doing things and improving my life/lifestyle. Part of that education was learning how to assess and evaluate if the glass is half full or completely empty when making big decisions. Also, the freeing power to say "NO" and not feel guilty about it. For a person with a spirit of giving and wanting to help people, saying "NO" can be difficult but sometimes necessary. Why, because those are the people that other people often take advantage of.

I am one of those people, like so many others, that have lived a life wanting and trying to make life better for the family generations coming behind us. Part of that means helping to open doors for more and better opportunities. Another huge piece of that is steering them away from life's pitfalls. I am convinced that this book represents both of those directions. It's also a lifetime collection of what I've learned and now know. One of the things it offers is to shorten the learning curve away from the consequences of bad decisions. That's accomplished in part by highlighting and putting a spotlight on the difference between everyday decisions versus transitional decisions and the effort level needed to deal with those differences. Transitional decisions have the power to turn a person's life in different directions.

As we individually travel down our life path, at different times those paths will lead us to a place of some common realizations; that life can be very difficult. I see life as the ultimate type of game with winners and losers. It's seldom static but more like always throwing things at us. Some we catch, some we dodge, but some will knock us down. When you start to compare the similarities of living to some difficult sports, it changes your focus on dealing with some life issues that we all must face from time to time.

When you start to recognize and understand the different nuances, challenges, and foundational rules of life and some sports, it only becomes the starting point for getting better at dealing with and playing them. Another example can be certain math problems you've placed in the hard-to-do column.

The real key to getting better is to learn how to break those things down in ways that give you a competitive advantage. Life, sports, and the math problems will still be hard, but with your competitive advantage they start to get easier for you because you are learning what to focus on and better ways to deal with them.

This book covers many of the issues of life we all are forced to deal with: things like redirecting a person's life when they find themselves going down a wrong path, how to preserve and protect relationships, how well are you transitioning through life, how to get ahead, and so much more. It chronicles my adventures, misadventures, decisions, and lessons learned; many with anecdotal stories.

It was originally directed towards the Black culture in an attempt to get us to stop sleepwalking through life. However, this book will appeal to people of all ages, backgrounds, and life experiences with its' simple inspirational messages.

My simplified Reader's Digest version of life goes something like this; you're born, stuff happens, then you die. The longer you live, the more stuff that happens. While nothing in that statement is untrue, the "stuff" is anything but simple, it represents the very essence of who we are in every way imaginable.

The stuff is how we start off in life, everything we've done, said, and acted out along our life's path. It's all the people we've met, the relationships that might have been built-up, and or destroyed over time. It's also our family ties, close or distant.

The stuff is also how we've supported ourselves, thus resulting in our lifestyles and the social networks we are associated with, our close friends, and others. That stuff is ultimately how society sees us and will judge us at life's end; our legacy; our "DASH." The dash that I'm referring to is the line between the birth and the death dates that will be on our tombstones. That little line, albeit small, represents our entire life lived which makes it huge.

Each of us is living through and managing the stuff in our lives. My life and my legacy are represented in part by this book; thus, the title, *"**Stringer's Dash**."*

The subtitle, *"Every life has value and a legacy to pass forward,"* is something I feel extremely strongly about.

I believe that every human life has value, in part because God told us that He placed value on us in the books of Matthew and Luke in the Bible. I believe that there are no ordinary people because each one of us is different and special by divine design. While no one is ordinary, there are people who have done extraordinary things with some of their life's work.

Don't think for one second that celebrities and/or the rich in society are the only ones that have stories worth telling. True, they have bigger platforms thus the capability of reaching more people; however, each one of us, while living our life's "Dash," have stories to tell with the possibility and capability of enriching someone's life. We just need to believe that truth and let our stories be told.

CHAPTER 1

-WHY THE BOOK? – WHY NOW?
Fulfilling a challenge and a promise..

Somewhere back in the mid 90's I attended a NAACP fund-raising dinner that turned out to be the genesis of this book. The keynote speaker for the event was a young Black man that had recently written a book on Black culture. While I don't remember all the points he made that night, there was one that haunted me for years.

He compared a sports analogy to why Black people have struggled as compared to other ethnic cultures. Perhaps part of the reason his example got seared into my brain is because the sport he chose was track, the one I love more than most. He said, "Imagine two cultures running the mile, one is running the mile relay while the other is running the mile. Who do you think is going to win?"

His example painted a very vivid picture for me. The answer was obvious, the culture running the mile relay will win every time; here's why. The mile relay is run with four racers. Each one runs one lap around the track then passes the baton until the fourth runner completes the mile. By contrast, the culture running the mile alone has no help. They pass the baton to no one; they start and finish the race by themselves.

What I believe he was saying is that we as a culture don't help each other like we should or could, and that typically within the Black culture each generation has to run their own mile. Be that as a culture in general or within our own families, we pass nothing or little forward.

When I left that event, the more I thought about the point he was making, the more I saw the truth in it. He also gave other examples to give weight to what he wanted his audience to understand and digest. That night I personalized his truth and challenged myself to pass something forward to my family with my life and or lifestyle; I just didn't know what.

During the speaker's presentation, he gave examples of some of the things we don't pass forward, things like wealth, businesses, and experiential knowledge. The one that was the most troubling to me was the experiential knowledge. What that said to me was that we don't even pass forward the knowledge we've learned or gathered, as we live our lives, to our family members or others that are coming behind us.

Years before that fundraising dinner, I did an experiment once that went exactly like I thought but was still troubling to me, nevertheless. My first wife and I bought a house on the side of town she grew up on. It was a nice house, and we got a good deal but the interest rates at that time were very high.

It's now about two years after the house purchase. The loan interest rates at our bank came down three percent. We refinanced our loan balance from 30 years to 15 years and our house payment only went up $8.00; knocked off 15 years and the monthly note went up less than $10.00. We felt pretty good about that financial maneuver.

At that time, I belonged to a predominantly Black church that had recently bought the elementary school I attended growing up. It was a major effort to convert the school into a church. That meant that the church Trustees (which I was one of) had a lot of work to do.

This was the experiment. At one of those scheduled work details, I told the story of our house refinancing to see what the response would be. At the end of my detailed account of the time and money saved, there was about 20 seconds of total silence followed by the work assignments handed out for that project. There were five of us in the room. There was not one inquiry as to how my wife and I made that happen, not one.

While driving home, I remember thinking that if I had mentioned something about one of the Motown singing groups coming to town, we would have been talking about it during the entire work detail. Those types of topics were not off limits. We like social events.

Leaving that fundraising dinner, I thought about that experiment. I also started thinking about some things I knew to be true and troubling about some of my people; some things I had experienced firsthand. The one big one that jumped out at me was that some of us don't like to talk about things of substance, particularly things of a financial nature. That one really stood out because at that time, I had a job working around mostly White people. One of the things I first noticed was that they talk about financial issues all the time. If someone got a new car or house, they had no problem discussing the cost, the down payment, the interest rate and where they may have gotten it.

Sometimes, when overhearing these discussions, I would try to imagine how a similar money discussion might play out with some of my people. First, they might look at you like you had lost your mind for asking about something they deemed so personal. An inquiry about money matters could also put you in a position to get your feelings hurt or just straight cussed out.

In the years that followed my initial desire to pass something forward, I thought that perhaps I could write a book detailing some of my victories, losses, and things I have learned along my life's journey. This was almost as a default because I had no real wealth, other than insurance policies, or a business to pass along.

To that end, from time to time, I would find myself thinking about a book project and making notes to myself that perhaps one day might inspire a chapter or two in this book that never seemed to quite go away. Over those same years, I would hardly mention the project because I didn't want the pressure of people asking how the book was coming along. Only a very select few knew that this was bouncing around somewhere in the back of my mind.

Now it's Thanksgiving 2015, our son's family is up from Indianapolis for the holiday. They alternate spending two holidays here in town: one-year Thanksgiving, the next year Christmas. Our Daughter-in-law is from Indianapolis, so the alternate holidays are spent there.

During that visit, I decided to call a family meeting. I had some things I wanted to share, especially with the grandkids. I wish that I could say that I had some great revelation or some voice from above told me to do this, but it wasn't like that at all. I simply felt like it was time. I was thinking about the challenge to myself to pass some things forward and I thought that everyone was now old enough to understand and appreciate what I wanted to talk about.

Part of my intention for the meeting was to help them understand that as they were changing by getting older, their challenges and their world would be changing also. I wanted to remind them that their responsibilities would be a lot different in the future they were marching towards than the ones in their youthful past. To that end, I also wanted to give them some tools to use and indicators to look out for to better navigate some of the uncertainties that would be on their horizons.

My plan was to communicate the things I wrote about in the chapter, "**How a mentor changed my life.**" Some of that chapter speaks to the importance of relationships in our lives and how best to preserve them. Also, the importance of honesty, not just from a legal and societal perspective, but the value of being honest to one's self when difficult times come, and they always do in this world.

Another point I wanted to make came from something I read about President Jimmy Carter concerning doing your best. I was going to broach the honesty issue with a story I heard within a Pastor's sermon one Sunday morning in church. He talked about Michael Jordan's *"Breakfast Club."*

The story was about how the basketball player for the Detroit Pistons, Joe Dumars, caused Michael Jordan of the Chicago Bulls to make changes in his life. Those changes were the impetus for him going from "Goodness" to hall of fame "Greatness."

In 1989, Jordan started working out with his trainer focusing on strength training and weights. His hard work motivated his teammates to join him. Most of the workouts were early in the morning before their regular practice sessions. Jordan would always show-up with a cup of coffee in hand. Thus, the gathering soon became known as the "*Breakfast Club.*"

This was the foundation for Jordan's six titles, six Finals MVP run. Michael knew that what he was previously doing was not good enough. Once he figured that out, he changed things to improve his chances of accomplishing his dream to become world champion. Michael experienced a life changing "Significant Emotional Event." I explain those types of events in the chapter "**Transition.**"

The impact or significance of the "*Breakfast Club*" has many life applications. The Pastor that Sunday used it to ask the congregation the question, "What is the Joe Dumars in your life?" The implication being, "What is your weakness or addiction or sin that is keeping you from being the person that God has created you to be?"

One of the things I saw in the story was the impact of honesty and hard work. Jordan was honest to himself and admitted that he was not strong enough to deal with Dumars in the critical fourth quarters of championship games; that was half of the change. The other half was addressing the problem to achieve the outcome he desired.

President Jimmy Carter has authored over forty books, one of them is *"Why not the best?"* In this book, he talks about the influence Admiral Hyman Rickover had on his life; one being to always do your best.

Admiral Rickover, the "Father of the U.S. Navy's nuclear submarine program," once interviewed James Earl Carter Jr. for a position to work with him on a nuclear submarine program.

His last question of the interview was this, "Did you do the best that you could when you were at the Naval Academy?" His answer after careful deliberation was, "No." The Admiral then turned his chair around so that his back was facing Carter and never said another word. The interview was over.

Mr. Carter got the job and went on to become the 39th president of the United States. He never wanted to answer "No" again if that question ever presented itself again. Did you do the best that you could?

My planned summary to the grandkids was going to be sim-

ple but profound. This was it, when you are faced with difficulties, first, look to yourself and be honest about the role you
may have played in the situation. Second, assess and evaluate
what it will take to get the result you want. Third, no matter
what you do in life, always do the very best that you can. It
does sound somewhat simple, but in truth, when you are up
against possible life-changing events, it can be anything but
simple. I touch on this in the chapter "**Transition**."

We were about twenty minutes into the meeting when a
family matter surfaced, and we had to break camp. The opportunity to meet again never presented itself before the holiday
weekend was over.

Now it's the winter of 2016. Every season of every year, I
identify projects for me to work on. My winter projects for
that year were, (1) regrout the downstairs bathroom off the
foyer, (2) paint the office. I always keep some kind of project
going because I'm very hyper and like to stay busy.

By the end of the second week in February, my two projects
were completed. For some reason I didn't want to add another
winter something to do. I felt a sense of calmness and directed my thoughts in a totally and somewhat unusually different
direction. I wanted to physically do nothing. I can't remember
another time in my adult life that I set aside time to do nothing. What I felt I needed and wanted to do was think, just

think. I told my wife, Renee, that I was going to take the last two weeks of the month to do nothing but think about Fred Stringer.

To think about my life in its entirety, things I've done, things I've wanted to do but were yet undone and some of my triumphs and remorse. Basically, my legacy in general made up the component parts of who I am now. This conversation happened on Monday.

My son and I try to always talk on Sundays. It's Tuesday, the day after I had that "Think" conversation with Renee. The phone rang and it's my son, Kevin. My first thoughts are that something bad has happened back in Indianapolis because we generally only talk on Sunday.

He opens up by asking me if I have ever thought about my legacy. I got goose bumps, partly because I was relieved that there was nothing wrong, but I think mostly because I couldn't believe his question. The fact that he asked me about something I had just set aside time to do was a little eerie. My reply was that my legacy was the only thing I was going to think about for the next two weeks.

He went on to ask if I remembered the family meeting back at Thanksgiving, I said, "yes."

He said that he had never seen his children that captivated by a conversation. He continued, "You know that book you would sometimes mention."

I said, "Yes." He then reminded me that I was not getting any younger and that within five years, I might not have the energy to take on a book writing project. I said, "Thanks for the age update."

The last thing he said was a game changer for me. He asked if I would take on the challenge of writing that book and make it his Christmas present in 2017. Although I had reservations, mostly because I had never done anything like this, I accepted his challenge and started writing the first week in March.

Now, the two weeks I had felt a new type of calmness about was suddenly replaced with a sense of anxiety and a deadline urgency. The set aside chill time of thinking about me is now the time I used to try and figure out how to start a new venture, writing a book about me.

Although I had been thinking about this subject for years now, I struggled with how to structure it. I knew that I didn't want it to be a religious type of book but rather more from a secular perspective; that much was clear to me. The thought that haunted me the most was simply this, when people finish the last chapter would they feel like it was a waste of their time or not! For me that meant that the reader had to come away with some things of value for them. I felt like just a simple chronological history of me from birth to now, would not be good enough.

When I started identifying the things I didn't want the book to be, my direction forward started to take form. This was the book structure I finally settled on.

I would trace my life story through events and talk about topics I have formed strong opinions about. I also felt that by mixing in stories about some places I've been, things I've done, things I've been exposed to, and lessons learned along the way, would paint the best picture of my legacy.

I determined that even though I'm not rich or famous, I have lived a full and sometimes interesting life. My mother once told me that you can even learn from a "fool" if nothing more than to not be foolish. I truly believe that everyone has a legacy worth sharing. I had a young man tell me once that he loves talking to older seasoned people because he always learned something. He went on to say that when an old person dies, it's like burning down a library. While I didn't want this to be about religion, I personally pray about everything that I do. I asked God to give me confirmation and guidance if this project was in His plans for me.

That spring after a few weeks of writing, I went to visit a friend of mine, Jim LaCivita. He asked if I would come work for him. Jim owned Deer Creek Golf Course in Hubbard, Ohio. He knew that I had worked several years at a golf course after I retired in 2004. I said maybe next year because I had too many irons in the fire at that time. He asked what had me so tied up. I told him that I was writing a book. He was the first person I told. People that know Jim, know that he can be a bit of a "smart-ass," so I wasn't sure what his response would be. His face shifted into a serious look and said, "I want a copy of that book when you finish." I promised him a free signed copy. Not one "smart crack," not one hint of a giggle, this for me was the final validation that I could and should write this book. Jim's words meant a great deal to me.

I never had the impression that Jim was very religious, but I knew that the Lord could use anybody at any time. This for me was the confirmation for which I was praying. Unfortunately, Jim passed away that fall which made me even more determined to complete the book and make good on my promise to him even though it would be posthumous.

The "**WHY THE BOOK**" was the culmination of that NAACP event and the challenge to myself of wanting to pass something forward to my family, my legacy. The "**WHY NOW**" was the fact that I'm getting up in age and the push from my son to capture my life's story in print. Were it not for his challenge, I might still be waiting in the starting blocks to go forward with this project. The promise of the book for Christmas 2017 was missed due to family health issues and

Kevin understood. I assured him that I would present a finished book to him one day; I was smart enough to not attach a date.

CHAPTER 2

- HOW DO YOU KNOW WHO YOU KNOW?
Understanding the power of time..

We live in an era of instant gratification, a time when data about things, people, and events are coming at us all the time. Anything we want to know is at our fingertips with just a single push of a button.

Let's examine the information we get exposed to and that we gather on our own about people in the media like athletes, politicians, television, and movie stars we've come to know, or do we know them? I ask that question because how well can we really know someone that is not in our personal circle, people we interact with on some regularity? The reality is, we think we know them quite well, particularly the ones that are standouts in their chosen careers. This is an attempt to shed some light on this topic and examine some cause and effect.

"You only have one opportunity to make a first impression."
How many times have we heard that! While that is true, in the
grand scheme of things, what does that really tell you about
a person? We should be very glad that there is little truth in
saying *"You only have one opportunity to make a lasting impression."*

There's a good reason you are asked to present your resume
when applying for a job. While your first impression interview will have some impact, your life's work and accomplishments will count for so much more.

Your resume tells a better story as to what you've done over
a period of time. The resume does not tell the whole story of
you, but to a possible employer, it begins to paint a picture as
to where you've been and the potential of how far you might
go within their structure.

One of the things all humans have in common is that we are
all associated with a name, with most of us it's our last name,
the family name. Where we differ is the value we place on that
name. The Bible has this to say about the subject, *"A good
name is more desirable than great riches; to be esteemed
is better than silver or gold"* (Proverbs 22:1 NIV). In other
words, a good name should be sought after more than riches
because it is more valuable. Esteem means to regard with re-

spect; prized.

I understand what the Bible is saying because we've all seen examples of people with great wealth that society has rejected and has no respect for. However, there are times when I hear a story or comment about the pitfalls of wealth, and I'm reminded of something a friend told me years ago. He said, "It's true that there is no guarantee that money will make you happy, but it does allow you to look for it in better places."

Most of us have been reminded of who we are representing when our behavior slips outside of the family's values or guidelines for proper conduct. It could be by a parent or some other family member safeguarding the family jewel/ their name.

Whether you have inherited a family name that is well respected, that you want to build on, or one you are not proud of, it is part of your legacy. What went on before you is history out of your control. What you do with your name now/your legacy, is all on you.

This is probably a good place to introduce you to a formula I ran across many years ago that has helped me be aware of some of life's truths. There are many things that I have held on to because I've recognized its' value, things that were either said in conversation or perhaps I saw on T.V. or read somewhere, like **P/T = R; perception over time equals reality**.

PERCEPTION: It's how you see or perceive someone, or something based on your interaction or information gathered on them. Our perception of things is being processed and molded continually as we live our lives. It's not something you have to think about, it just happens.

TIME: There have been many things written about time. One of my favorites is a quote by Henry Van Dyke; *"Time is too slow for those who wait, too swift for those who fear, too long for those who grieve, too short for those who rejoice, but for those who love, time is eternity."*

However, **TIME** in this formula speaks to the length of time we've known about someone or something. Nothing vague or fancy, just good old fashion time; seconds into minutes, minutes into hours, days into months and so on.

REALTY: It's what you believe a person or thing to be based on, of certain factors and events you've observed or experienced over a period of time. Next, I am going to be analyzing people and how it relates to this formula.

Your contact with a person over a period of time has convinced you that they are who and what you have come to know them to be. Have you ever gone to a wedding and thought to yourself that it felt more like a pre-divorce ceremony? I know I have. The reason for my attitude was based on how I felt about one or both individuals. My reality of them was formed by my perception of them over time. That perception convinced me that the marriage was doomed. **P/T = R.**

The major component in this formula is **T** (time). It takes time to really get to know someone. What you've learned about a person and how you've gathered this information was either experienced or perceived from them over a period of time. The longer the time, the more confidence we have in what we feel this person is about and who they really are.

However, with that being said, we all have seen things that cause that formula to blow up in our face. An athlete, a T.V. star, a politician, or even people within our circle that we had labeled one way turns out to be someone altogether different.

Unfortunately, there are too many examples of that, but for the most part the formula holds true. Even if you question the formula's value, you can't stop it from how we see and evaluate people. Why? Because our minds are constantly working and processing data. The people processing mechanism in our brain is always turned on.

So, you might be asking yourself, how can I make this work for me? I'm glad you asked. For starters, knowing that this process is constantly going on, puts you ahead of all those who are not aware of it. It also should make you aware that all your actions are being evaluated either consciously or sub-consciously by those you encounter. In other words, you are always painting a picture of yourself everywhere you go.

A real advantage to understanding this formula is this, it allows you to rewind the clock and look backwards at events when you realize something has changed, particularly when things are changing for the worse. This is important because while living our lives, most changes are slow, subtle, and happen over time. These are the changes that sneak up on you, but other people notice the change.

When something major happens, most of the time we are aware of the changes that might have occurred as the result of that event or series of events. Often time the subtle changes are reactions to things that are going on around you.

Take the workplace for instance, perhaps you've had a difference of opinion with a co-worker that causes you to see and maybe treat them a little differently. Or maybe you have a new boss because there has been a change in your area, or you have moved to a new office. Either way, there is a different feel to your space. While it is obvious to you that some changes are taking place, what may not be as apparent is the changes that are happening to you.

There could be some things going on within your family or social life, perhaps your circle of friends is changing. It could be a matter of trust, you told someone something in confidence and you found out that they shared that information, thus mishandling your trust in them.

As a result, you tell yourself that you won't make that mistake again. So, what you are saying is that you no longer trust that person the way you once did, that is clear to you. However, what is likely to happen is that you start to question the trust you have in a lot of people. This might result in you being a little less talkative or perhaps a little withdrawn from how you usually are.

One day you see someone you haven't seen in a while. Not long into the conversation they make a comment, "Are you O.K.?" The words catch you off guard because in your mind, there might have been some small changes in your environment, but you feel that they didn't change you.

When others see things in you that you don't see, instead of dismissing them, see this as an opportunity to reassess some things in your life. Rewind the clock, look backwards, review past events big and small and honestly evaluate how they may have impacted you. Understanding this formula will help you figure out what may have happened and why some people now see you differently than you see yourself.

While the time in the formula is still the major player, it can be tricky. What I mean by that is while most of the time it is seen as how people label other people; you can't forget that no one spends more time with you than you.

You see, you have also labeled yourself. That's why people that have not seen you for a long time, sometimes make observations about you that don't correspond with how you have labeled yourself, it can be a shock to the system. Their reality of you is different than the one they previously had. It might be the result of subtle changes over time that you did not notice but to a fresh set of eyes are very noticeable.

One Sunday morning, in the middle of our pastor's sermon, he begins to tell a story about a certain man and woman that had a chance encounter at a convention in Las Vegas. The woman is beautiful, impeccably dressed from head to toe. She walks with pure elegance, long flowing hair bouncing off her shoulders with each graceful step she takes.

The man is equally impressive, looking like someone of means, a CEO or perhaps a successful business owner. They both happen to be leaving early and reach the door at the same time. The man is taken by her beauty and presence. On the other side of the door, he presents her with a bold hello and question. The question is "Will you sleep with me tonight for one million dollars?"

This stops her in her tracks. Startled, unbelieving what she just heard, a bit angered but also a bit curious, she replies "Are you talking to me?" He looks her straight in her eyes, says yes and repeats the question.

She looks around to see if there is anyone within hearing distance and replies, "What do you mean?"

He begins to detail the terms. "One night only, no strings attached."

She thinks about it for a few seconds, repeats the terms, and even thought to herself, "I have never done anything like this before." She says yes. He went on to explain that he had a penthouse suite in this very hotel.

They begin walking towards the bank of elevators on the far wall. A few steps in, he turns to her with some new numbers, "How about a half-a-million?" She stops, ponders, and agrees.

A few steps more and he asked, "How about three hundred thousand?" She's starting to get annoyed now but keeps walking and agrees.

Now they've reached the elevators, one last chance to negotiate, "How about two hundred dollars?"

She turns, puts her hands on her hips in total disgust and says, "Two hundred dollars, who do you think I am?"

His reply, "We've already determined that, we're just dickering on the price now."

The pastor's message was on character, those things you do in the dark when you think no one is watching, and he also emphasized that your talk needs to line up with your walk. While I agree with the points the pastor was trying to make, my reason for telling the story is related to this formula. Although you see yourself one way, your actions or behavior may say something different, causing people to see you in a way you never dreamed possible. This could especially be true with a first impression encounter.

Change in life is going to happen, it happens all the time. Some good, some not so good, and some bad, but change is a big part of life. We should not be afraid of change, but we do need to recognize it and properly process the impact it will or could have on our lives.

Even things we might see as a good change need to be put under the spotlight. Nothing is ever truly free, most things come with a price. This formula can help you through some of these evaluations. It can be a good tool to have in your pocket. I'm not trying to encourage anyone to be a super nice person 24/7, not at all. Just be yourself because over a long period of time, it's nearly impossible to fool people; what's in you is going to come out. You don't squeeze an orange and get apple juice.

When things are running smooth and pretty much going your way, it's easy to be who you think people want you to be. Most of us know what to say and do in most situations to make us look good and acceptable. However, that knowledge is sometimes put on the shelf when we are put under pressure. It's often in those tight, pressure-packed scenarios that the real you show's up. Those moments can change a person's view of you in a heartbeat, sometimes for the better, sometimes not. Just know that this formula is always in play. However, because the heart of it is time, over time you have an opportunity to change things if you choose to.

There was a time in my life when this formula was very much in play, and it worked against me. This story is not easy for me to tell but if it can help lift someone from a dark place, then it will be worth telling.

Having graduated from a small school on the small side of town in a relatively small city, it's safe to say I wasn't very worldly. Racial issues were not that obvious where I lived and went to school. I mostly knew about them from what I saw on the T.V. news casts and what I read in the newspapers and magazines.

However, my experience level for the racial divide in our country was about to change in a big way. After graduating from high school, I volunteered to join the United States Air Force. The Air Force was about to send me to the Deep South. That experience would impact my life to this very day.

I first went to Lackland Air Force Base in San Antonio, Texas for my basic training. It of course was different from what I was used to but not bad. My next assignment was to Keesler Air Force Base in Biloxi, Mississippi for technical training; BAD. What I experienced in a few weeks on that base would take me nearly three years to recover from, it was nothing physical but rather mental and emotional. I'll talk more in detail about that experience in the chapter, "**Growing up in the United States Air Force.**"

When I left Mississippi, I was a very angry young Black man. My anger was like a powder keg or a rage that I felt could blow at any time. Also, when I left Mississippi, I made myself a promise that I would not take any crap from anybody for the rest of my life. Unfortunately for me, I meant every word of it, and it cost me a lot.

My next assignment was up north in Duluth, Minnesota. A decent base but I arrived with an attitude, a bad one. Most of the time people saw me as I wanted them to see me; a fun-loving easy-going guy, but just underneath the surface, that powder keg had a short fuse. On base, I got into several fights and had two Article 15s (that's disciplinary action and paperwork in your file) against me. That status was not good for making rank and climbing the ladder in the military. My future was anything but bright.

Then something happened that made me want to start the

change back to who I really was, inside and out. Towards the end of my second year in Duluth, I got married and my wife came to live with me off base. My attitude started to change for the better. That rage I used to feel within me was fading fast. I was almost Fred again. While that part of my life was changing, there was another part that was not. You see, the powers to be, my superiors up the ranks still had me down on paper as being smart but somewhere between a hot head and a troublemaker. This was a big problem.

A few months after we were married, I got orders to go to a base that was isolated / remote, Saglek Bay Labrador, Canada. When those orders came down, my wife was two months pregnant with our first child. She moved back to Ohio to live with her parents while I moved on to my new assignment.

My flight to Labrador was long which afforded me a lot of time to think about my future and my future family. I thought about the child my wife was carrying and about the environment within our home that I wanted that child to experience. To me, it meant that I had to make the change that had started, complete!

On that plane ride I made myself another promise, this one was a lot different than the one I made leaving Biloxi and I wanted to be even more dedicated to it. The promise was this; I would be the best person I could possibly be. I said that I would dedicate myself to being a positive role model for my child and my entire family. Seglak Bay was going to be a fresh start for me, none of these people knew me.

When I was processing in, the personnel airman called me up to the counter. He said, "Here take this," and handed me a file. It was the Article 15s that I received in Duluth. He said, "These are not supposed to travel with you, they stay at the base you came from. Somebody back there must really not like you."

I thanked him and said to myself, "Thank God they don't travel." That just confirmed what I was already committed to do, change.

I arrived with a new attitude, anxious to let everybody know who I really was and what I was about. Not long after I got there, I had two extra jobs, then three. Everybody knew I was hard working.

It wasn't long after that I was written up in the Air Force newspaper (The Eastern NORAD region; Aerospace Defense for the Eastern United States) for being Airman of the month and quarter (Jan – Mar 1969).

The last paragraph of the article reads as follows; "The unit commander, Maj. James J. Kelly, praised the young NCO's military bearing, appearance, poise, maturity and self-discipline."

How's that for a turnaround?! You see, over time coupled with a new beginning, I was able to create a new reality of me within my new surroundings. The formula was now working to my advantage.

Not long after I had been discharged from the military and started to settle into my new family life, I had a time of reflection. I looked back at some of the things that had occurred and discovered something that caused me to make a change as to how I was going to approach certain situations. What I uncovered was, the people I quickly learned to hate in Mississippi, guess what? I had turned into one! Although it wasn't for a long time, for a period I was just like some of them; judging people based on things that should not matter like skin color, rather than an individual's merit or character. I was as wrong as they were.

I have since tried to live my life to make sure that I never sink to that level again. I got confirmation that I had moved in the right direction through a conversation I had with my son the first time he came home from college. He said, "Dad, I'm glad you didn't raise me to be prejudice." At first, I was taken back by that comment because I couldn't remember having those kinds of talks with him. Then I started to recall some talks about treating people based on how they treat you and treating people like you want to be treated but not a big, long dissertation about Blacks and Whites.

He went on to say that some of the Black students he had met on campus were very prejudice. It was White folks this and White folks that everywhere they went and how much that bothered him.

I know we had conversations about being a Black man in a world that is predominately controlled by White people. It was for the purpose of being aware of it and making the necessary adjustments, like no one is going to give you anything. If you want something, you'll have to work for It. Our talks were not about hatred.

Enough on that subject, there are plenty of books on Black and White issues. While that's important, I want this to be about other things that impact our lives. I'm going to conclude this topic on the formula with two stories about two individuals that crossed my path while working in the engineering building at my old job.

These two people found themselves in similar situations relative to the formula but had two very different results. These are real people with real names but for the purpose of these illustrations, I will rename them Dick and Jane. Dick was out of his second year, and this was Jane's first at the workplace. Dick was a young Italian pretty boy. He was very sure of himself, a bit narcissistic, a hands-on kind of guy, and sometimes a loner because he stayed to himself for the most part. We worked in the same engineering area but reported to different bosses. He was smart and over time we became friends.

I learned that he had a large pet snake when he came to work one day with a bandage on his hand. He said that he was exercising the snake by letting him crawl away then pulling him back. The snake got tired of the drill, snapped around and bit him. I learned this less than one week before he was to get married to his high school sweetheart, he called the wedding off. According to Dick, he couldn't tell who hated him the most, his fiancé, her parents, or his. Her parents and his parents were longtime friends. This was not a good time in Dick's life.

While I didn't know everything he did at work, I knew he was responsible for building and debugging injection molds. I knew that we had a mold tryout area that was mostly run by technicians. I say mostly run by the technicians because Dick liked to go down there and get more involved than most engineers. Like I said, he was a hands-on guy.

One day I was privy to some information that was about to have a major impact on Dick's life. I told him we needed to talk and invited him to lunch. At lunch I asked him how was the job going. He didn't say fine or bad it was more like so-so. It was then that I said, "I don't know what's going on with you but if you don't start making some right now changes, you are going to lose your job. They are making a case to fire you."

It was then that he shared what was happening and I offered some ways that he could possibly start to change some things to turn his situation around. As it turned out, it wasn't that he was doing a lot of bad things, it was more of a perceived attitude that was not playing very well within his group. He knew that he was not always on the same page as his boss, but he didn't think it was bad enough to lose his job.

Lunch was over, he thanked me and immediately began to make changes. While the changes were enough to keep his job, they were not enough to overcome all his perceived baggage. Dick relocated to another state but still within the corporation.

The biggest difference he made was not his address but his attitude. He changed his formula. Even though he was not aware of the formula, he knew that he needed to make sure that his perception was in line with what he wanted his career to look like. You see, Dick was always a hard worker and wanted to do well within the organization, he just went at it the wrong way.

Jane was an attractive, proud African American young lady with high ambitions and big dreams. She was involved with several organizations and business ventures. I was a supervisor in engineering when we met. The corporation had a mentoring program to help the African American college new hires get acclimated to corporate life; to help get them off to a good start. I volunteered to be a mentor in the program, and Jane was my new mentee.

Over time I learned more about Jane. She was bullheaded, set in her ways, wanted to do things her way, didn't have enough respect for authority, wasn't a high achiever and didn't like to get up early. She had come to earn my nick name for her, "Drama." I gave her full access to me and there were many late-night conversations discussing her issues. Her formula was in play, and it was not good. She was being perceived in ways that would make it impossible to climb the corporate ladder. I finally suggested that her best hope was to leave Ohio and get a fresh start.

I went out on a limb and asked someone I had built a good relationship with to hire her (it was still within the corporation but in Michigan). He was heading up a new program and was in the process of building his team. After an interview and several conversations, he agreed to give her a job. I saw this as a new beginning for Jane. It wasn't very long before my phone started ringing again with some of the same old issues. Her new boss, my friend, was not treating her fairly, much like the situations that had gone on in Ohio. She assumed everyone was picking on her. I spoke to my friend, and he told me point blank that she was not measuring up and if things didn't change, he was going to fire her.

I shared that conversation with Jane and offered some suggestions that might turn things around. I also asked her a question, "What has been the common denominator in all the places you've worked within the corporation?" She got quiet and didn't answer so I answered for her. "What's different is the jobs and the supervisors but what's the same is you, your attitude, your excuses and the results." I suggested that the first turnaround needs to start with her. The next time I heard from her, she was in Atlanta working as a teacher in a school system.

In summary, Jane was forced to leave the organization and Dick moved within the organization and went on to become pretty big cheese, Superintendent the last time I checked. Dick likes to tell the story of how I saved his career.

The simple truth of these two stories is this. Dick took responsibility for how he was being perceived and made the effort to change. **P/T=R.** Dick changed how he was being perceived and over time, people's reality of him was positive. Jane never changed her formula. She was always making excuses for her situation.

Knowing about this formula will do you little good if you

don't do an honest assessment and make necessary adjustments during the times you evaluate your situation. Perhaps you've made some mistakes in your life causing people and society to label you a certain way because of it. Over time you can relabel yourself. Or maybe you've disappointed or emotionally hurt some people you care about and would like to turn things around. Just know that over time the fix is possible. Time can be your friend, or it can really work against you. Your formula is in your hands.

Know and understand this; TIME IS ALWAYS IN PLAY; PLAY NICE BOYS AND GIRLS!!!

CHAPTER 3

-TRANSITION

Wake up! Sleepwalking through life can be costly.

During our early parenting days, when our kids were very young, visits to their various doctors were regular and seemed to be often. As I recall, most of the magazines in the waiting rooms were family friendly with fun things and funny stories to read about. One I liked and got hooked on was *"Highlights,"* and I still enjoy it to this day. The magazine always had a picture puzzle, and I loved to see how fast I could finish it.

I remember on one occasion; I picked up some magazine that had a brain teaser in it. In those days, I saw myself as an intelligent adult. So, a brain teaser in a kids magazine, how hard could it be? I took on the challenge. It went something like this, "What animal starts off on four legs, transitions to two legs, then transitions to three legs?"

That teaser proved to be more than my brain could handle, I couldn't come up with the right answer. When I saw the animal on the page with all the answers, I remember thinking that the question was a little misleading, then immediately reminding myself that this was for kids, they didn't need to be technically correct.

The animal was us, human beings. When babies start getting around, they are crawling on their hands and knees (four legs), then we standup walking and running (two legs), later in life our walking is aided with the use of a cane (three legs). Another way of looking at this riddle is how we transition through life, the aging process. Transition is change. That's a very simplistic way to look at it. My grandmother would sometimes say, "It's a bad wind that never changes." I thought she was talking about tornadoes and hurricanes but perhaps she knew that one day I'd be writing on the subject of "Transition" and that statement would have relevance: clearly a lady ahead of her time. Everything that touches our lives can create transitional periods; crossroads that might require life changing decisions.

Our lives are made up of three fundamental parts; yesterday, today, and tomorrow; the past, the right now, and what's to come. The question is, how well do we transition from one block of time to another. How are we changing or reacting to change as we take on the challenges of living everyday life?

This is a serious question because how our minds process those time slots and how we react to them determines how we live our lives. The human brain is so dynamic and sophisticated, it is capable and often does give us feedback on all three-time zones instantaneously.

Yes, as life comes at us, we are always living in the moment of time (the right now), but we are constantly getting feedback that sounds like, "Remember this, remember that, and how is this going to play out down the road?"

Actually, that's a good scenario because when you only live in the moment with little to no regard for past or future results, you roll the dice between good and bad, success or failure. In sports like in life, this process is weighted heavily on the situation.

In sports, when you are in the moment of doing something you've done before and the outcome the last time was favorable, your confidence that the next outcome can and should workout good for you again is usually high.

However, if the opposite happened the last time you were in that position, then it is better to try and dismiss those thoughts and tell yourself, "This is a new moment that can have a better result," like a quarterback throwing an interception on his last pass attempt. Athletes call that having a short memory, so they can better focus on the task at hand, the right now.

For most of us outside of the sports arena, remembering bad things that happened in the past can be very beneficial in the right now and future. These failures or hurts or whatever constitutes bad for you, if properly remembered and applied to future decision making should lead to better outcomes, wiser choices, and the possibility of a brighter future.

Good things that happened in our past are easy to recall and feed on, I believe that the not so good things in our past hold the possibility of more value. Many of life's difficulties or failures have the potential to make us stronger and better. The key is how we handle those times and events. It's been said that life is made up of 20% of things that happen to you and 80% of how you react to them. While those numbers might not be exact, it seems like the greater impact on our lives is in the reaction to events and situations.

When I was younger and would hear about someone committing suicide, it seemed to stay with me for a period of time. I would try to understand and ask the question, "What happened?" I had a hard time getting past the fact that when you only have one life to live, why would anybody throw it away?

Sometimes the suicide victims would leave a note or letter

of explanation of their decision to end their life. Often when the reasons were made public, I would find myself in a state of disbelief. It was hard to understand sometimes because some of the reasons they felt devastated to the point of death, were things that people dealt with all the time. That 20% event that made them unable to see a future perhaps would have been a mild steppingstone for some others.

It might have been a relationship break-up or the loss of a job that they processed one way, while some others might have handled that same situation differently and quite possibly would have come out on the other side a stronger, better, and wiser person. For any situation you can imagine, there will be varying results because no two people are alike. I have a friend that has attempted suicide several times, it was not because of situational circumstances but rather due to a chemical imbalance in his body. God made us uniquely different by design, thus causing us to process things differently.

Our constantly transitioning lives are always lived in the moment. You might have your thoughts and eyes on the past or future, but we literally do live in the moment. Those moments lead from minutes to hours to days culminating into years, then one day when someone is wishing us Happy Birthday, we say to ourselves, "Wow, am I really that old?" You start to ask yourself, "How did I get from the long-ago things remembered to now; where did the time go?"

Truth is, it went in moments, I have had many birthdays that I asked myself some probing questions. Questions like, "What happened to those goals I set for myself to be completed by the time I was thirty," or "Now that I'm a year older and hopefully a year wiser, what does success mean for me now and am I getting closer to it?"

I'm now 69 years young. I know what you're thinking but I like phrasing it that way, it makes me feel better. I'm looking backwards and trying to assess what I perceive to be the good and the not so good, while figuring out how those things have impacted and shaped my life. I first thought that I could review it in decades, ten-year segments; zero to ten, ten to twenty and so on. However, I quickly discovered that there had to be a better way that would have more meaning; a way that would be easier to see and evaluate transition periods in my life.

I came upon something that I thought made sense, **events.** We all live our lives through the events we are transitioning through and it's an easy way to associate time and age. Pre-school, high school, military, marriage, kids, divorce, and a litany of other things. How did I transition through things that happened in my life? Doing it this way gave me a lot of options as to how I could look at different events, those that happened to me and others.

I think that it's worthwhile and healthy to look back at times and events in our lives to establish baselines on how certain things turned out based on our decisions. You can learn from good end results and learn even more from the ones that were not so good. The key is understanding and knowing that living life is a process; the more you learn, the better you should get at decision making.

As we age, there are many signs along the way that let us know that things are changing or have changed. Our clothes no longer fit us like they used to, we might not have as much hair to fuss over, and we find that some of our hair color has changed to a shade of gray. We reflect from time to time where we are on our trek towards retirement because things are changing. Some changes we try to ignore, some we attempt to fix, while others we just accept. For the most part, those are our three basic options; ignore, fix, or accept. There are billion-dollar industries that are in place to help fix or change us as we transition the aging process.

We're getting older, but we want to stay in shape, so we join a health club and get a personal trainer. We pick up unwanted weight, so we bounce between one dietary plan and then another. We're getting older and our face is showing signs or there are parts of our body that we think would look better either bigger or smaller, so we seek plastic surgeons. As we age, our health begins to change or fail making us more reliant on doctors, hospitals, and medicines. Though this can be a mix bag of complicated issues, most of the time it beats the alternative, the ultimate transition, death. If your heart is beating, you are making your way through the aging process which obviously is of vital importance.

I'm going to shift gears and talk about some things I feel are equally important, the decisions we make along our life's journey. Our transition as we experience life has many moving parts that determine what our lives are like as we go through our aging phases. Every situation we encounter, good, bad, or indifferent, has the potential and or opportunity to be a transitional point in our lives. How you transition is how you live your life; how you live your life has a lot to do with your quality of life; your quality of life has much to do with your happiness in life.

This could be the result of or in spite of money, things, success, failure, or perhaps your attitude towards acceptance of things. Do you see the glass half empty or half full? How you think speaks volumes as to where you are emotionally, intellectually, and where you are in your maturity development.

In the Bible, in 1st Corinthians, the great apostle Paul wrote a letter to the people in the city of Corinth, scolding and teaching them about the dos and don'ts of Christian behavior. One of his statements spoke of transitioning into maturity.

In chapter thirteen verse eleven, Paul said this, "When I was a child I talked like a child, I thought like a child, I reasoned like a child. When I became a man, I put childish ways behind me (NIV)." The opposite of what Paul was saying is that if you are in your manhood/mature years and still acting and making childish decisions, something is wrong and needs to be adjusted; you are not transitioning very well. Unfortunately, we all know people who seemingly can't get out of their own way. They made bad decisions in their youth, early adult lives, and then in their forties and fifties, and they are still making the same mistakes.

I have a very good friend that is in prison right now. This is his third time being incarcerated; he has spent a lot of his adult life locked up. We went to high school together and in our senior year became close. He introduced me to my first wife, was best man in our wedding, and is Godfather to our son. He is very charismatic, a life-of-the-party kind of guy. He could take any situation and find something funny in it to make you laugh. People would tell him all the time that he missed his calling, that he could be a stand-up comedian.

With that being said, he had one glaring character flaw, he

didn't want to work for the things he wanted. Though he had many opportunities with what most people would call good jobs, the money wasn't coming fast enough going down that forty-hour per week road. This resulted in him becoming a bank robber. When he ran out of money, he would rob a bank and get some more. Through our many conversations, I learned that with the money from one of those robberies, he was going to open a bar in New York City. When that didn't work out, he resorted to robbing banks again.

There were many problems with his choice of vocation, one being his physical description. He has light skin and stands six feet three inches tall. When the F.B.I. looks at the security film of his robberies, it's not long before his name comes up. I guess there are not a lot of people with his description robbing banks.

After a prison stint, it never took him long to land on his feet. One such time he was living and working in Atlanta, Georgia. He was doing quite well. He had been married for about a year to his former boss, living in a nice house in a very nice neighborhood when I paid him a visit during a business trip. While in Atlanta, we saw each other twice. The first night he invited me over for dinner to meet his new family and the next day we went to lunch.

It was during lunch he told me something that bothered me

for a long time, it was the answer to a question I asked him. I inquired, "What were you thinking just before you went into these banks, did you think you were going to get away with it?"

He replied, "No!" He also said that most people locked up for bank robberies, if they were honest, would say the same thing. It wasn't a question of would he get caught, it was only a question of when. He told me that robbing banks was close to insanity, it makes no real sense. Then he laughed, probably because of the look I had on my face.

That look represented surprise and maybe even shock because his answer was the polar opposite of what I expected. I suppose my expectation was more in-line with what I have seen on television; where the bank robbers plot and scheme then come up with an elaborate plan that they totally expect to work, thus beating the system and to never get caught. The reason his answer bothered me for so long is because it meant he had no problem with going back into the penal system.

This made me think about something my brother in-law from my first marriage once told me, he also had done time in that system. He said, "Once you learn how to jail, there's nothing to it."

Sometimes when my friend's name comes up in conversation, someone might suggest that he is institutionalized. I'm not going to label him, but I will say that his mindset and behavior is something my mind has difficulty processing.

Your past can be a tremendous tool in helping you move forward. I say can be because while the past is a ready reference and a learning opportunity, we don't always take advantage of it. It might be asked, "Why?" When you are transitioning properly, that three letter word should only haunt us once per incident or situation because we should be learning from our mistakes. We all make mistakes and generally the people who don't repeat or compound them are the ones who move forward in positive directions.

It's like in golf when you hit a shot into the woods, all golfers have done it with varying next shot results. In those moments, we think about the other times we were in the trees and what happened next. You remember that miracle shot that somehow landed on the green and your playing group looked at you like they were seeing Bubba Watson as you poked your chest out and smiled saying to yourself, "Yea I'm that good."

Then your mind quickly transitions to that time when you tried that miracle shot and a whole lot of bad things happened; greeting your group on those occasions saying, "Yea I'm that stupid." They call them miracle shots for a reason, another term often used is low percentage shots because most of the time you're going to fail.

Now your past has given you options, the smart choice is to admit your mistake, take your medicine, chip out, and minimize the damage. Another example is how some people handle bad financial situations, sometimes they are not at fault but often they are. Either way, there are decisions to be made. When you are at those crossroads, the choices you make can weigh heavily on your future. If self-inflicted and not too serious, you can sometimes tighten your spending belt, get out of trouble, and move on learning from your mistakes.

When financial situations are more drastic, bankruptcy might be the best option. As bad as that might sound, there are many examples of people using that tool and going on to become wealthy and successful. Others file for bankruptcy and continue to struggle because they don't learn from the past and keep falling into the same traps. When you make the same decisions, coming out of bad situations, your transition to something better suffers.

As we make our way through this maze we call life, we encounter many opportunities and things happening to us along the way. We get jobs, some get married and have kids while others choose to remain single. For those of us that chose marriage, we sometimes refer to singles as the smart ones! The transition from being single to being married is filled with so many twists and turns. Your local library has shelves filled with books offering help on how to navigate that sometimes treacherous journey, I'm going to add my two cents on something I discovered along my path.

Most experts agree that the two biggest problems facing married couples are communication and finances. These two marital issues are obvious to most people and can be springboards to many other problems, I've discovered one that is not as obvious but can be equally problematic. I call it the "*Being Number One*" syndrome. I believe it's something we are born with that never leaves us, and as we age and mature (or not) it takes on different forms but is always there.

We start developing this trait early in life, you see it in young children. Often time when they don't get their way, they can publicly display their disapproval, quite loudly sometimes. What children are expressing is their version of not "*being number one*" at the time they want something or want to do something. Their need to come first is not the main priority at that moment and they don't like it.

As children grow up within families, they are constantly vying for attention and this gets played out in a variety of ways, some healthy and some not so much. Jealousy and life-long problems between siblings can occur plus a host of other things like personality disorders.

Now let's look at the transition from being single to getting married. You are now transitioning from me to us, this is a very big deal with the mind psyche. Nearly from birth, it's been me, me, me, now it's us. Transitioning between those small two-letter words can bring on a mountain of new thought patterns. What I believe makes for the best results in a marriage is when the "*being number one*" on the list is transferred between the spouses. The husband makes his wife "number one" on his list, and she makes him "number one" on hers. They are both number one on a list but now it's the us list and not the me list, it's all about priority.

I also believe that marriages get in trouble when one or both individuals stay number one on their own list, causing acts of selfishness and not properly looking out for their mate. The Bible states that when a man and a woman get married, they become one flesh. Along with that, they should also become one priority, each other's.

Another huge marriage transition is becoming parents, more pulling away from you "*being number one.*" In another real sense, you go from being a student in life lessons to becoming a teacher. How that transition evolves can run the gamut between children growing up and becoming president of a company to those locked down in our penal system. Parenting is very serious business; I will express more of my views on the subject in the chapter "**Family.**"

There are many transitional dynamics within marriage, a big one is divorce. Whenever I get the news of a couple divorcing, the analytical parts of my brain seem to get activated with the how come, the what for, and the basic what happened? This is especially true when a couple has been married a long time, twenty years or more. When some of the "What happened" comes out, it sometimes gets even more surprising. That's because to someone on the outside looking in, the "What happened" balanced against the length of time they were together, seemed to be something they should have been able to handle and work out.

The focus may have been on the job. Now that one or both are retired, that forty-hour-a-week away from each other, is now spent together. That means togetherness time is now 24/7.

It could be that the two expended their energy and resources on raising a family and now the nest is empty or perhaps someone's health has changed for the worse and the burden of care giving has never been the other person's strong suit. Then there's the obvious and most common, the introduction of a third person into the marriage, an affair.

Often in a marriage that doesn't work out, it's not because one person is good and the other one is bad, sometimes you have two good people with good intentions that just have a hard time making it work and that becomes the issue.

It's kind of like two exact magnets, put them together one way and they will stick to each other, put them together the wrong way and they will repel each other. The magnets individually are perfectly fine, however, misapplied, they don't serve their intended purpose. Marriage can be like that, two good people having a difficult time making it work and that's a big part of what marriage is, work!

Let's look at the divorce of marriages of twenty plus years, being a witness to these events over my lifetime has given me some strong opinions as to what might have happened. While the contributing factors might have been different, there seems to be a thread that is common to most, at some point the marriage stopped growing. The calendar was marking time but in the past the marriage stopped moving in a positive direction.

People that study these things for a living probably have some big technical term for it, but I just know that somewhere back in time, the focus moved away from husband and wife to other things and failed to transition back. Some may have been intentional while others were perhaps gradual as daily life happened and for a long time, the changes were hardly noticed or ignored.

One such gradual incident happened to me and my first wife. It was after the birth of our second child, Nicole. My wife was working for an insurance company as a claims adjuster when she got pregnant. She liked her job and was good at it. She took leave from work a few weeks before the estimated due date.

After our daughter was born, I convinced her to quit her job to stay home to raise our two kids. My wife being the 24/7, stay at home homemaker was my vision of how things should be and at that time, she was in agreement.

After about a year into our arrangement, I came into the bedroom one night and found her crying in bed. I asked what was wrong and she gave me the patented first response, "Oh nothing." Crying was a very long way from nothing for me, so I pressed for a serious conversation.

She opened up and said, "You don't talk to me." Now I'm sitting on the edge of the bed in silence trying to figure out what that means. I've never been much of a talker. I would generally come home from work, ask how her day went, ask about the kids, eat, and start working on some project; I always had something to work on. I hardly ever initiated conversation about my job. I felt that I wasn't talking to her any less than I always did; I was confused.

The thing is, while I hadn't changed her, her situation had changed big time, and I failed to recognize and adjust to all the transitions that was happening within our family dynamic. I knew we went from one child to two, I knew that she was no longer working and had given up all the independence that went along with that. However, I didn't understand the social aspects of what the job provided, being around her co-workers and some had become close friends.

What I came to realize is that these were the people she was talking to for eight hours a day, five days a week. She could deal with my low conversation output on the weekends because she knew that Monday was coming, plus I talked more on Saturdays and Sundays.

We talked about the pros and cons of her going back to work. We decided it was something she really wanted at the time, and I gave her my blessings. That next day she called her old boss, and explained she was ready to come back to work if there was an opening. There was a place for her, and they were very glad to have her back in the office and we made the necessary adjustments at home; "*Happy wife*," you know the rest.

We had been living a lifestyle that was the number one reason for marriages getting in trouble, lack of communication. After that discovery, even though she was back at work and probably didn't need it, I initiated more conversation with her.

With all the transition opportunities awaiting the twists and turns of first-time marriages, for those persons that get second and more chances, there are even more transitional possibilities. That's because in most cases, there are more people that have a stake in the marriage, stepchildren, X spouses, X in-laws, more friends and so on. Though the multipliers might change, the mental approach to recognizing and properly reacting to transitional periods should not change.

On the path to getting a driver's license, you must first have a driving permit. To get the permit, you must pass a written exam on the rules of the road and part of the test is on the road signs. Knowing what those signs mean and properly navigating through them can keep you out of dangerous and possibly deadly driving situations.

Understanding the interactions between marriage and the power of transitioning can also be very helpful. Learning the signs of a transitional event allows you to put a label on it, thus warning you to slow down, proceed with caution, possible dangerous curve ahead.

Transitioning through marriage is kind of like the gear shift on a car with an automatic transmission. There are four basic functions: Park (**P**), Reverse (**R**), Neutral (**N**) and Drive (**D**).

Either your marriage is moving forward (**D**), and things are going well, the bond between the spouses are getting stronger; or it's in neutral (**N**) O.K., not great but not bad; or it's in reverse (**R**) things are moving in the wrong direction heading towards bad; or it's in park (**P**) possible separation, possible divorce proceedings.

It should be noted that reverse (**R**) is right next to park (**P**), one action or bad decision away from each other. Though not board-certified to give marital advice, I would like to offer a suggestion that might help to save a relationship.

A great tradition celebrated around the world is the beginning of a new calendar year, you often hear about and probably take part in making New Year's resolutions. That's a time I generally review the year that we've turned the page on and think about the possibilities of the one in front of me. Now that I'm older, I've learned not to make resolutions. My looking back mostly consist of thanking God for the portion of health that I still have and for bringing me through to see another year.

My marital suggestion is a simple one. Regardless as to how long you've been married, at least once-a-year, could be at this time or perhaps your wedding anniversary, ask yourselves some questions and evaluate how you and your spouse are transitioning in your marriage (a yearly assessment to consider possible adjustments).

Easy questions, do you feel the marriage is getting better or worse, then ask questions related to how you've responded. The real key is that you must be honest. This is not the time to try and please your mate, it's the time to show love by being honest with your mate.

One big advantage to doing this is that you are taking one-year snapshots as to where you are, hopefully avoiding the situation of looking back after long periods of time and possibly wondering what went wrong. Making small transitional adjustments are usually easier than the ones that have taken root and grown over the course of many years.

Society likes to mark transitional periods in blocks of time and events, the "Roaring Twenties," the 50s, 60s and so on. The events would include all our wars and war-like conflicts and things like when the *"Hippies"* ruled. They have also assigned names and traits to the time periods we were born in like *"Baby Boomer*s" and *"Millennials."*

Sometimes our legal system helps us to recognize when we are going through a transitional period. Things like the legal age to vote, drink, and one that got my attention, when you are considered an adult in the eyes of the law. That one stood out to me because I knew from that point on if I did something stupid, I could go to the grown-man's prison.

Because we make up this society and thus help to determine the norms (what is normal acceptance), we have bought into many, if not most of these labels and thinking patterns, like sometimes making a big deal when the first number of your age changes. It seems like one of the most troubling age transitions is from 29 to 30.

My first wife's transition from 2 to 3 was epic. When I look back at that period in our lives, I can see some things that I've come to label as "Life Formulas" in play; **"perception over time equals reality"** and **"people get used to what you get them use to"** were the two and they were about to be challenged. She was attempting to make a paradigm shift within our family dynamic. When she turned thirty, we had been married for eleven years and had settled into a comfortable lifestyle. My **reality** of her over that period and **what she had gotten me used to** was set and very acceptable to me.

My wife and I got married when we were young, too young by some social standards. I was twenty-one and she was nineteen. She was a mother for the first time at twenty-one and gave birth to our second child at the age of twenty-five. My wife had taken on serious adult responsibilities at a time when most people are exploring life and enjoying their youth.

She and I both made those decisions with our eyes wide open at that time, I say it that way because sometimes you question past decisions that at a certain time in your life you were very sure of. Now she is turning her back on her twenties and the thirties are staring her in the face, perhaps marching towards the thirties, looking back at the twenties, and wondering what she might have missed out on.

It's Friday in late July 1978, she is now thirty years and two months old. I'm working the afternoon shift which puts me home a little after midnight. I get off work, pull in the driveway, and push the button on the garage door opener. The door goes up and reveals a room with a lawn mower and other outdoor tools but no car, my wife's car is missing. I have two first thoughts; either this is a case for the Police and my insurance company because the car has been stolen, or my wife is out somewhere and it's going on one o'clock in the morning and she somehow forgot to mention it to me.

She returned home at 2:00 a.m. and explained that she was out with some of her girlfriends, some married and some not. It sounded reasonable but because I got no prior notification, I was not happy. Three weeks later a similar scenario happened, but this time it's a Saturday night and she gets home even later.

I remember waking up that Sunday morning, the sun was shining with the promise of what should have been a pleasant family day. However, pleasantries were the last thing on my mind; I had some business to handle. A good family friend used to always say, "either you handle your business, or it will handle you," this was one of those times for me.

When I got up, I woke her up and asked her to meet me at the kitchen table for a two-person meeting. There was no "Good Morning, "and she was not greeted with my usual smile. She probably thought this was not going to be a fun way to start her day, and in a very short period of time it became crystal clear that there would be no fun at this meeting.

When she entered the kitchen, I was already seated. My wife joined me at the table. I began to talk as she sat in silence. While I don't remember my words verbatim, the monologue went something like this: "I'm well aware that you recently turned thirty, you reminded me of that several times over the past few weeks. Those mentions of the first number in your age changing from two to three, coupled with last night makes me feel like you are possibly looking for something. Perhaps things you think you missed out on or maybe a lifestyle that is different than the one you currently have, either way here is my position, and it is non-negotiable."

"If I ever get off work again and come home to an empty garage that I wasn't expecting, you are going to find yourself with a lot of free time on your hands. The time you currently spend cooking our food, cleaning the house, and time spent with me and the kids in our home. All that time will be available for you to find whatever it is you are looking for; however, you will have to set aside some of that time to meet with your lawyer because you'll need one for the divorce proceedings."

I also mentioned that I would be fighting for custody of the kids, I'm remembering that conversation without the cuss words that I'm sure were sprinkled in somewhere.

That was the beginning of a difficult day, however, by the day's end we were on the same page and went on to a wonderful marriage of twenty-two years. Unfortunately, that was ended when she lost her battle with breast cancer.

There's a term that I ran across concerning transition and change that I found to be powerful and true, the term is "Significant Emotional Event." It's been said that real changes mostly happen when this event occurs, something that shakes you to your core enough to make you or gives you the courage to make a change in your life. There was a significant event in my life that caused me to get serious about my walk and commitment to serving the Lord.

My daughter was about five years old, one evening she wasn't feeling well and was running a high temperature. We took her to the local hospital emergency facility. After the initial exam, it was decided that my daughter should be admitted. Forty-five minutes later, she was in her assigned room but looking and acting extremely different. My daughter was unable to talk, and parts of her body were distorted. I looked at her chart and immediately went out to the nurse's station and got somewhat indignant. They had noted on her chart that she was retarded, that's how fast her condition was deteriorating.

That night felt like the longest of my life. They brought in a team of doctors and nurses to monitor her throughout the night. They would come in every hour on the hour, with charts and a pin flashlight looking in her eyes to see if her brain was starting to swell, they had warned us of all the possible scenarios if that were to begin to happen. Each hour after the exam, they would give my wife and I the thumbs up. We prayed all night. At some point during that process, I did something I should not have done, but sometimes desperate people do desperate things. I made a deal with the Lord, that if He spared my daughter's life, I would be serious about serving Him for the rest of mine.

After a four-day hospital stay, and a variety of tests that never answered what had happened to her, we were blessed to bring our daughter home. The Lord spared her, and I have been serving Him from that day to now. I sometimes wonder what my Christian life would look like if the Lord had taken my child. That's a story for another time, but that event was a "significant emotional event" for me, and I transitioned accordingly.

I was up late one night surfing television channels and ran across an infomercial on smoking. I was a smoker at the time and wanted to quit, so I put my skepticism radar on alert and watched the program. I don't remember the product they were trying to sell but they made a point in the presentation that got my attention, and I packed it away in my knowledge/information toolbox. They said in simple layman terms that your brain is divided into two parts, intellectual and emotional. They went on to say that in the average person's brain, the intellectual portion is developed between 8% to 10% while the emotional is between 70% to 80%. The point they were trying to drive home was that whenever your brain gets into a debate over a subject you are emotional about, most of the time, the emotions will win out; 10% vs 80%.

They pointed out that the reason people have a hard time giving up smoking is because it's emotional, it makes us feel good, it relaxes us. We read the warning on the packaging that "Smoking can be hazardous to your health," and we light up anyway. Intellectually, we understand what that means but we like doing it.

That's where this term comes to bear and will be a major player in anything emotionally you are trying to move away from, "Significant Emotional Event." The key and the ultimate difference maker are the word and the meaning of "Significant."

I figured out that there are two measurables/metrics to use to know when you have experienced one of these events, (1) you can point back to the event, (2) the change that was made because of the event was permanent (you never revert to what you had moved away from). I use terms that reflect the past as the litmus test for a reason, (point back and was permanent), that reason being the difference between an event and a significant event. I'll share a personal example.

I wanted to stop smoking because I knew that it was not good for my health. Knowing some of the statistics on annual deaths attributed to smoking and lung cancer, I made several attempts at quitting with minimal success. At some point, I went back to the habit of smoking. I knew about this term, "significant emotional event" and thought that the events of one particular night (playing the card game pinochle with friends) was going to be my event to finally stop smoking.

We were playing pinochle at my house. Usually on these occasions we would just play cards, smoke cigarettes, and other things. However, on this night I had some hard pepperoni logs that I sliced and served with cheese and crackers. The game broke up around 3 a.m. I cleaned up before going to bed, now it's about 4 a.m. Suddenly, my stomach started cramping. I began throwing up, and it escalated quickly. I felt so horrible, I thought I was dying. At one point, the pain was so severe, I was afraid I wasn't going to die because I thought death would be less painful.

Thanks to God I survived, and later that day, after some welcomed sleep, I promised myself that I would never subject my body to anything I ingested that night. Surely, remembering the pain of that night would offset any urge I might ever have to smoke. This time I stayed off longer than I ever had before but eventually started smoking again. That painful night became just an event, not one that was significant enough to make me quit for good.

Today, I am thankful to say that I am a non-smoker of thirty years. You see, I did finally have my "significant emotional event." One night, while surfing the T.V. channels again, I ran across a medical program on smoking. The presenting doctor showed a dramatization of the inner workings of our lungs. It showed the inside of a pair of lungs coated with a tar-like substance that had built up from smoking. It also showed small Artesian-like springs spraying and washing the inside of the lungs. He explained that this is the body's way of keeping our lungs clean. Then he stated that each time you smoke a cigarette, you shut those springs down for eight hours.

What the doctor said next helped me even more with my

decision and ability to quit. He said, "That's why it's never too late to stop smoking, because when you do, those springs start working again, cleaning and moving you towards healthier lungs. That one-hour program with that one diagram and explanation was my emotional event. Each time I thought about smoking, I thought about stopping that cleaning action for eight hours and I determined that it was not worth it.

You see, I liked to smoke, (emotional) but I liked the idea of clean lungs in my body even more (emotional). Now the emotional body factor overpowered the emotional urge to smoke and got on the same page with my intellect which allowed me to transition into a non-smoker for good.

Years later, I know that it truly was a "Significant Emotional Event" because I can point back to the event/that medical program on smoking and the change was permanent. It was the same with my attitude toward serving the Lord, my daughter's hospital experience was the event and I'm still in the church.

I once watched a television program on men abusing women. They said on average, women that experience physical abuse will go back into that situation seven times before they finally leave their abuser. My take on that is the first seven times no matter how severe the abuse or what promises they made to themselves or others that might have resulted, they were just events. However, at some point after seven, they had an encounter with a "significant emotional event" and made the change to something better.

Finally, I wanted to broach this subject on transition and present a few examples because it's a very fluent, impactful, and integral part of living life. Most things we do on a regular basis almost become instinctive, we don't think about it, we often just react as time marches on. I call this "SLEEPWALK-ING" our way through life.

One of the major problems with "Sleeping" at times of decision making is that we make those decisions without putting enough thought or weight into any down-the-road implications, the focus is mostly on that moment/that situation. We simply want to get through it, get it out of our face, and move on. The problem is some of those decisions could have been life transitional/ life changing. Down-the-road they could develop into an opportunity missed or something much worse than the original situation you were trying to resolve.

There's a question I ask myself when I'm about to make a decision I've deemed to be important, possibly transitional, it's "WHO'S WALKING THE DOG?" It sounds simple, but the back story has relevance for me, that phrase is my alarm clock to wake up, not a time to ASSUME or to be CARE-LESS.

One summer, a neighbor on my street died. He lived alone.

His brother came up from Florida with his dog to deal with the issues of his house. He was in his late 80s and in dog years so was his dog.

Most summer days I like to do yard work in the mornings or late afternoons to avoid the midday sun. The mornings were also the time my late neighbor's brother from Florida liked to walk his dog. That's how we met and shared morning conversations. The odd way he walked his dog was noticeable. Most people walk their dogs on the sidewalk only, but not him. He did walk on the sidewalk, but mostly all over the neighbor's yards, only stopping short of going up the steps onto the porch. After the third day of observing his dog walking style, I asked why he was walking through people's yards. His answer became my sleepwalking alarm clock. He said that because his dog was old, he just hung on to the leash and followed wherever he wanted to go, basically the dog was making the decisions and walking him.

One day, about two weeks later, I had conversations with two neighbors about him and his dog. The first was a neighbor showing me videos on his phone from his house cameras, asking if I knew who the trespassing man with the dog was. It was the new pair from Florida, so of course I said yes. The videos showed them walking in the yard with the dog peeing and pooping at will. He complained that he didn't like it even though he carried and used a poop bag with the dog.

The second conversation came with a picture of the dog in the neighbor's garage. Apparently, he got loose and was in there for hours before they called the dog warden to remove him. I explained that I knew who the owner of the dog was, but the incident happened a few days prior. He said that he followed up with the dog pound and found out the dog and owner were reunited.

The next morning, we had our conversation, but this one was different. I shared the complaint of the neighbor with the videos. His response, "But I get up the poop." I just looked at him. He then asked me to tell the neighbors that it would never happen again. I did, and he and his dog were never seen walking on the street again. I missed our morning talks.

My takeaway was two parts, first, no matter how well he cared after his dog, that one day his dog wandered away. He was careless and could have lost his dog forever. Second, he assumed that because he was cleaning up behind his dog, the neighbors would be O.K. with it, they weren't. The owner was careless and made wrong assumptions.

When approaching the crossroads of making big decisions, everyone needs a type of alarm for us to wake up, pay attention, and start due diligence for what's about to happen. For me, it's "Fred, who's walking the dog?" don't be careless or assume.

I wanted to put a spotlight on this dynamic so that we would wake up at critical decision-making times. We need to be more aware of things happening around us, put the proper label on it, process it, and respond appropriately. Life and transitioning through it is like a Merry-Go-Round ride that you only get off when your music stops, the ultimate transition at life's end. The ability to quickly identify transitional events will allow for an early start to making necessary adjustments thus helping to make the ride through life a little merrier.

CHAPTER 4

-GROWING UP IN THE UNITED STATES AIR FORCE

It's not your start but rather your journey that will define you.

There is a nine by eleven-and-a-half-inch plaque, black frame trimmed in gold, hanging on the wall in the office of our home. The plaque represents three years, six months, and twenty-three days of my life, it's a framed certificate of my honorable discharge from the United States Air Force (USAF).

Sometimes I look at the plaque like any other picture that hangs throughout the house. Then there are many other times it represents so much more, a badge of honor, a sense of accomplishment, and a mixed bag of memories, memories I've labeled as the good, the not so good but not bad, the bad, and the make folks think that I had lost my mind ugly.

Big bold letters with impressive script across the top, it reads, "Honorable Discharge" with the seal of the Air Force just underneath. Then it goes on to say "From the armed forces of the United States of America. This is to certify that Frederick H. Stringer, SGT USAFR was honorably discharged from the United States Air Force on the 23rd day of March 1972. This certificate is awarded as a testimonial of honest and faithful service." Signed by James G. Stephanidis, Colonel, USAF. It looks good on the wall and represents one of the most influential periods of my life.

I wish I could say that the sight of the plaque swells up pride of patriotism, but it doesn't. Much like when I go to sporting events, and we are asked to stand, remove our hats, and face the flag while our national anthem is played. Sometimes when I'm in those moments, I think about one of the military lifers I reported to in my last duty assignment, everyone called him Sergeant Mort.

He once told me that when he attends events and our national anthem is played or sung, he looks at the flag and always cries. I never asked why, and he never told me why. I imagined that by him being a career military man, he probably knew people who made the ultimate sacrifice defending that flag.

During the Viet Nam war, most people either personally knew or knew of someone that was killed over there. When news of those deaths filtered through our neighborhood, we always viewed it as tragic and unnecessary. You would hear things like, "Why are we over there fighting a war we don't understand?" or worse, "Why are we over there fighting the White man's war, and we are back here being treated like shit, second class citizens?"

While I'm not qualified to represent the mindset of all the Blacks during this period, I believe like me, most of us were not volunteering to go fight and possibly die for this country and flag. Most were forced to go to war by our legal obligation to the military. However, on the other side of that, if you knew people who willing went to fight for our country and lost their life, the sight of the flag of the United States of America would mean something very special. That was how I explained away some of Mort's tears.

Reflecting on my growing up time in the Air Force, I can see the many faces of Fred or the changes I went through. I believe that it is impossible to do a hitch in the military and come out the same person that first went in.

I was leaving a culture that represented a comfort zone of eighteen years for me and trading it for the unknown of military life away from home. We lived on the east side of town called the Sharon-Line. My neighborhood, growing up, was primarily Black and it went on like that for several miles in every direction. There was one White married couple that lived on our street, the Rollers. Mrs. Roller was a close friend of my grandmother.

It turns out that my childhood living situation was unique. I say it that way because it wasn't until I was grown and looked back at it that I realized how special it was. We lived on one side of the street with my grandparents directly across the street from us. On the left side of them, facing their house, was my mother's brother's house and family and on the right was her sister's house and family. My childhood was spent living with my parents, one brother, and two sisters surrounded by my grandparents, aunts, uncles, cousins, and neighborhood friends. Everybody looked out for each other. The adults would make sure your parents knew about anything you did that was out of order. It was a magical time.

My pre-teen summers were spent between fishing trips with my family and all-day sessions at Baily Park that was at the end of our street. I never tired of spending time there because it was a young person's wonderland. There was a large baseball field with concrete bleachers that hosted organized baseball games for adults and other teams. Under the bleachers were rooms and tables that summer counselors would use to provide board games and crafts for us kids. There was also basketball, swings, teeter totters, and my favorite, a large sand box that I thought was mine.

My high school was small compared to most of the other

schools in town. While the student body was a healthy mix of Blacks and Whites, the teachers and administration were predominately White. We only had one Black teacher, Harold Davis (The Rock). My graduating class was made up of 74 Whites and 62 Blacks. There were some racial incidents at our school, but they were isolated and never amounted to very much. Most of the people, most of the time, got along quite well.

I graduated from high school in 1965. There was a lot going on in our country in the sixties. Racial tensions between Blacks and Whites were at an all-time high. While this was going on within our borders, we were engaged in a controversial war, a world away called Viet Nam.

These two issues were ripping at the very fabric of who we were as Americans. In those days, after you graduated, you couldn't just sit around waiting to find yourself. You had a very short window of time to decide what your next move was going to be because of the Viet Nam War draft. After graduation, all the males had to register for the draft.

You were facing one of three options if you were a healthy male; go to college because college students were exempt from the draft, go to the military, or leave the country. Well, there was a fourth, refuse to be drafted and go to jail. I had several options for college but felt like I needed a break from that school thing, so I said no to more schooling. Leaving the country or going to jail wasn't even a thought for me so I opted for the U.S. Air Force. I left for the Air Force on June 21, 1966. It was a non-stop series of firsts for me, mostly because the culture of military life was very different than the one I came from.

My first time away from home, the first time I felt totally responsible for myself. It was the first time I experienced loneliness surrounded by hundreds of people and the first time I challenged my manhood to step-up to represent my name and family, which came towards the end of my career. At the beginning and mostly throughout my career I was trying to get by, counting the days to hang the uniform in the closet for good.

Whenever I hear someone say, "It's not how you start, it's how you finish that counts," I think about my Air Force days. My start was kind of shaky, the middle got better but my finish was strong. I'm proud of what I was able to accomplish by the time I walked away.

If you were drafted, you were either going to the Army or the Marines for a two-year tour of duty. While volunteering for the Air Force was a four-year commitment, I felt it gave me better odds for survival. The Army and the Marines were literally on the front lines of the battle. They were experiencing the bulk of the war casualties.

Four years versus two but I viewed it as more than doubling my chances of coming home alive. I thought the Air Force would be an acceptable cocoon that would allow me to transition into adulthood and give me time to figure out what I really wanted to do with my life. It kind of worked like that; I grew up, but the experience wasn't anything like I had envisioned.

BASIC TRAINING; *San Antonio, Texas*

I saw the purpose of basic training as being three-fold. First, to test you physically with rigorous exercise to get you in shape. Second, to challenge you mentally and begin the process of stripping away whatever culture you came in with and replacing it with the Air Force way of thinking and doing things. Lastly, to identify your job for the next four years.

The physical part was easy, I was an athlete in high school and arrived in pretty good shape, but the other parts were question marks. Things started to get crazy for me within the first few weeks. One day I got an anonymous letter post marked from my hometown detailing some series of events. Supposedly, it was about what this person was seeing my girlfriend doing. No names were mentioned but they accused her of riding around in different cars with different boys. His final statement was this, "I'm not saying she's cheating on you but what do you think?"

Well, I started thinking all sorts of things, like how did you get my address, who are you, and what is the motive behind this letter? It took me all of one day to answer those questions. Not long before I met my girlfriend, she had broken up with her boyfriend who just happened to also be in the Air Force.

The first day in my dorm, I met a guy from my hometown. He went to high school with my girlfriend and was friends with her and her X. My conclusion was, this guy probably wrote his friend/my girl's X, mentioned that he and I met and was living in the same dorm. So, he only needed the return address and to put my name on the envelope. He knew me because we had a run-in shortly after I started dating my girlfriend. He came home on a weekend leave and it got ugly quick. However, that's another story for another time, but that answered all three questions. Once I sorted that out, the situation became comical to me.

There was one thing that letter helped crystallize for me, something I always felt but couldn't quite put a label on, I never liked nor wanted anything that wasn't desirable to other people. In other words, I liked things of value and was willing to work, fight, and sacrifice to obtain them. My girlfriend was a nice lady. She was pretty, and I saw value in her presence.

Although I wasn't arrogant, I was very self-assured. I didn't think anybody could take anything from me that I really wanted. I only saw this as a slight challenge, never a real threat, and that was in part because I didn't have a lot invested into the relationship at that time. I was in like, not love, by the way that girlfriend later became my wife.

A quick side note about some of my views on value. We've all heard things like, *"One man's junk is another man's treasure"* and *"Beauty is in the eyes of the beholder."* In other words, everyone has a different set of standards for assigning value. Two simple definitions; (1) material worth, (2) worth in importance or usefulness to the possessor. This small five letter word impacts our life and lifestyle in a variety of ways. I'll give you one example that helped shape my view on this subject.

When I got out of the Air Force in 1970, I went to visit my grandparents. They were in the living room watching T.V. After the hugs and kisses, I asked a question, "Why are you still watching black and white television?"

My grandmother's reply, "So it won't get stolen if someone breaks in, they won't take a black and white T.V." I could hardly believe what I was hearing. To me it was like saying, I don't want a beautiful wife because someone might take her from me, or I don't want a nice car because it might get stolen, or I could crash it. It just made no sense to me.

I asked her another question, "So, you don't have a color T.V. because you're afraid a thief will come in and steal it?"

She said, "Yes."

I told her that someone had already stolen it, and the thief was her. I said that she had deprived herself of enjoying color television because she was afraid of something that might never happen. I reminded my grandmother of this thing called insurance and the dangers of living her life in fear of things.

I mentioned before that I sacrifice to gain things of value, and my grandparents were sacrificing for fear of losing things of value. To me, that style of living isn't living at all, it's simply existing. I've never heard people say, "They existed life to the fullest." However, I have heard it said, "They lived life to the fullest." My point is this, make sure you have a healthy attitude about things you place value on. Your lifestyle will tell you who's in control, you, or your valuables. You simply must be brave enough to listen and adjust if necessary. By the way, my grandparents got a very nice color television the following week.

Back to my Air Force adventure, a week after my mysterious letter I had my first misstep. On a Saturday we were told there was going to be a G. I. party. All I heard was party. After working hard all week in that hot Texas sun, a party sounded good to me. However, the next thing I noticed was buckets, mops, rags, brooms, and cleaning materials appearing. Shortly after that, assignments were given out. You see, G. I. party is military jargon for an intensive, top-down, inside-out group cleaning of the barracks.

We were getting ready for a competition of sorts between barracks. The different barracks were referred to as sister flights. This was not the kind of party I had in mind. I got upset and walked out of the barracks down to a communal area that had a bunch of vending machines. It wasn't long after I got there, I was about to be even more upset. You see, I wasn't properly dressed to be outside. I didn't have on a hat or shirt and my t-shirt was not tucked in.

Out of nowhere, this Drill Sergeant appears and starts ripping me up one side and down the other. He asked what my name is, where did I belong, why was I improperly dressed, and it seemed like a hundred other questions. I need to mention that he was talking very loud and scary. I thought he was going to haul me off to one of those military prisons I had seen on T.V. After he figured he had sufficiently put the fear of God in me, he ordered me back to the barracks. My takeaway lesson from that afternoon session was two-fold. First, every Black person in a uniform is not your brother; did I fail to mention the Drill Sergeant was Black? Second, when you are in basic training, you better be where you are supposed to be.

Towards the end of my basic training time, I figured out why this guy had this attitude towards me. It wasn't as much a Black or White issue as it was a first timer versus a lifer issue. I felt like lifers saw us as part-time soldiers and were not going to go out of their way to bend the rules for us, I believe that to be a true statement in general. However, I was in basic training and hadn't even reached that part-time status yet. Therefore, I was seen as having no rights at all and should be treated as such.

My next misadventure took place a few days later and was huge. We were told that it was competition week with our sister flight and that we could be inspected any day. That meant that each day until we were inspected, someone would be excused from the hot sun's exercises and stay back in the air-conditioned barracks to let the inspectors in.

This was Tuesday, hot outside, and I was chosen to stay inside in case this was the day. I was incredibly happy for all of about two hours. When you come into the barracks, about ten steps in, off to the right, is a large latrine with urinals, toilets, shower stalls, and a lot of mirrors over sinks. I was looking at the tan line on my bald head when I heard this loud pounding at the double doors. I thought my heart was going to jump out of my shirt. Oh no, these are the inspectors. My hat was on the shelf under the mirrors. When I reached for it, I hit it and knocked it about fifteen feet across the room onto the floor. The pounding at the door continued.

I grabbed my hat and went into a half walk half run towards the doors. In my excitement, it must have been more of a run than walk because when I got there and hit the panic bars on the door, it flew open and just about knocked one of the inspectors over the railing. His hat flew off, and his clipboard went flying down the steps. If he hadn't caught himself with the railing, the inspector would have followed his clipboard. In the meantime, his partner is laughing so hard he is bent over with tears in his eyes. Now I've got one inspector gathering himself, while the other one is pointing and laughing, one looking extremely pissed off, and one looking like he had just seen something on America's Funniest Videos.

Now I'm looking at them with the door half open. Clipboard in hand, the inspector grabbed the door handle, and I jerked it out of his hand and asked if he was on the authorized access list. I was slowly coming back to my senses. That's the question you ask before you let anyone in. He said, "yes," and his partner started laughing again.

He walks inside. His face and ears are red, forearm starting to bruise up, and shouts to me, "Airman you better know everything you're supposed to!" When we first arrived at the barracks to start our training, one of the things we were given was a small book on Air Force protocol, chain of command, and some other military stuff. The information in that book was what he was referring to when he said everything I was supposed to know.

I knew this was going to be problematic because I had paid very little attention to that book. The first three questions he asked, I did not know the answers to. I guess he was starting to feel guilty about his choice of questions. So, the fourth and last question was, "Who is the president of the United States?" I got that answer right. They finished the inspection and gave me the report to give to our drill sergeant. I handed him the report when he came in.

He read it, looked up at me and asked, "What the hell happened?" We ended up with six demerits, three of them were the questions I missed. He looked back down at the report and said, "These are questions that are hardly ever asked." He asked me again, "What happened?"

I confessed to him the series of events. My drill sergeant didn't say another word, he just looked at me with a look I have never forgotten, a look of total disappointment. Our sister flight got four demerits; we lost the competition.

There were no consequences for us losing, it was for the most part a pride/bragging rights thing between the drill sergeants. As for me, I mentally punished myself because I felt responsible for our loss. When basic training was over, I left San Antonio with that look seared in my brain. I made a vow to never let anything like that happen to me again.

TECHNICAL TRAINING; *Biloxi, Mississippi*

My next assignment was some technical training, I was going to be a surveillance technician. This job was like an aircraft control operator except you don't help planes take off and land, it was designed to help keep the country's borders safe. Keesler Air Force Base in Biloxi was about to take "BAD START" to a whole new level for me.

Technical school was very regimented, all the classes were for a certain length of time which meant that new classes started at certain times. When you arrive in Biloxi, determined how long you would have to wait to start school. My gap between arrival and school was close to three weeks. While you were waiting, you are housed in a special area. What you find out immediately is that there is no sitting around watching T. V. or goofing off while you are in wait, there are eight-hour daily work assignments five days a week. Those work details were when the crazy started for me.

There is much to be done on a large training base like Keesler, a lot of housing units with grounds that need to be maintained and schools that need to be cleaned daily. Our barracks had people coming and leaving all the time because of the different school starts.

A typical day starts at 6:30 a.m., breakfast from 7:00 a.m. to 8:00 a.m., and reporting for duty at 8:30 a.m. Each workday begins with breaking starch, which means you must show up with creases in your pants. There are good jobs and bad ones, the good ones are cleaning the school buildings and classrooms because they're air conditioned. All the rest are bad because they are outside jobs in the hot sun.

The people handing out the jobs are airman that had washed out of one of the schools and awaiting a new assignment at a new base. These were people who needed something less challenging and now have a bad attitude. Your assignment was based on what these dropouts wanted to give you. I got some good jobs and some outside work.

My last week before starting school, we got a washout that was from the DEEP SOUTH. He made it clear from Monday on, the Blacks, all five of us, were going to be working outside.

Now it's Friday, we've been here for over two weeks, so we are familiar with all the outside jobs, and we are feeling good. Why? Because we know that all the outside stuff has been completed. The airman looks at his chart and does not know what to do with us. He said, "I'll be right back." He needed to go check with his boss. We light up cigarettes and kickback.

He came back with a smile on his face, "This is what I want you to do, draw an imaginary line down the middle of the street that goes around the building. Sweep the street from the middle to the curb. When you get to a parked car, sweep under it as best you can and."

The "and" was the last word I heard before my mind went blank. Before I knew it, I was in his face, pushing him with both hands, and telling him what I thought about him and his family.

I pushed him and accused him of being born out of wedlock. Second push, I told him he was having intercourse with his mother. The third push, I questioned his intelligence. By the fourth push he was having more sex with his mother. The next push put him on the ground. He got up and disappeared into the building where his boss was. I didn't know what was coming next, but I felt better.

Nothing happened, I figured he might have been too embarrassed to tell his boss that he had been pushed around by some Black guy from up NORTH. However, we did sweep the street. Now Friday is behind me and Monday starts my schooling or technical training. Over the weekend I move to a new building and get ready to start another adventure. The other four Blacks were still waiting for their different schools to start.

That last week before school presented some other misadventures for me. You see, there was also an evening job. People were coming on base, going into some of the barracks, and stealing mattresses. That meant that they needed people to pull dorm guard duty for a few hours each night. They would place a list in our barracks of the people needing to report for that job. That week, I missed showing up for two nights and was in big trouble the next mornings. I didn't figure out what was going on until it was too late.

I would come in from my daytime duty, check the list and plan the rest of my day accordingly. On those two occasions, I checked the list, my name was not there, I did other things. What I didn't know was that somebody had a second list that did not have my name on it, that's the one that was posted when I came in to check the list. After I left, they would post the real list with me on it.

My two failures to report for duty was passed on to my new instructors at school and others. They were told to keep an eye on me. However, it didn't take me long to win the instructors over to my side. They saw that I was smart and hard working. School was one thing, some people in my new living quarters were a different story.

You had to keep your room in a particular order, then there were also duties that were assigned for each floor. All the jobs rotated except mine. My job was always to clean the nasty latrine. People would piss on the floor, spit on the walls and circle it with a marker saying, "Don't forget this one Nigger." I wasn't just the only Black person on the floor, I was the only one on that wing.

After three weeks of that foolishness, I went to talk to the officer in charge of my building. He was a young red head Second Lieutenant. I pleaded my case to him. He looked up at me, lit a cigar, put his feet up on the desk and asked me, "So what seems to be the problem airman?"

I didn't want to believe what I was hearing. I was furious! I told him, "Sir, this is what the problem is about to be. When I catch one of these assholes doing this and throw his ass out of a window at a time of my choosing, then maybe you'll start to understand the problem." The next week I got a new job, but my latrine rotation was still more frequent than the others.

The first chance I had to return home after leaving for basic training was Labor Day weekend 1966, it was in the middle of my technical training. They informed us two weeks in advance that if we could show proof of round-trip tickets that would get us back in time for school on Tuesday, we could leave for the Holiday because school would be closed in observance. I was excited about the prospect of going home to see my folks but mostly to see my girlfriend. I purchased my tickets a week early and now I only needed to get a fresh haircut.

There was a lady friend of my grandmother's that had a grandson that was also stationed at Keesler at that time doing technical training. His schooling was much longer than mine. He was there when I got there and would still be there when I left. His name is Charles, and he was from my hometown. I looked him up the first week I got on base. We became fast friends and would hang out most weekends. He got round trip tickets too because he was anxious to get home to spend time with his girlfriend.

Charles had been downtown before and knew where the Black barbershop was, we decided to go the weekend before the Holiday. Charles had another friend that was also going home so the three of us caught the bus on base and headed downtown. We got to the barbershop, got our haircuts, and made our way back to the bus station. The Black people on base knew that it was not a good idea to be downtown after dark.

The bus station was an old house with the first floor gutted and converted for this business. It wasn't a huge space, but it had a large counter on one wall to purchase your tickets and some snacks that were stacked on the back wall. Two of the walls, opposite each other, had wooden benches for seating and the wall opposite the counter had two pinball machines against it.

There was a petite young White girl behind the counter and four elderly White men sitting on the benches across from us. We had about twenty minutes to wait before the next bus was scheduled for the base. I decided to kill my time playing the pinball machines. I told Charles my plan and went to get up. He grabbed my leg and suggested that I not do that. I looked at him, smiled, and pushed his hand away as I proceeded towards the machines. I noticed the conversation across the room had stopped because the room suddenly got quiet.

When I reached the pinball machines, the girl behind the counter said, "Those are not for you." I heard her say that, but my back was towards her, and I didn't think she was speaking to me. The next time she spoke was much louder and it was, "Nigger, I said those ain't for you." Now I know she's talking to me, so I turned to my left, went back to my seat never looking at her or the White men who still were not talking.

When I sat down, Charles put his hand on my knee and said, "I tried to tell you." I felt embarrassed, helpless, and anger but mostly anger.

Intellectually, I knew what racism and hatred was because I had seen it played out many times in the various media.

However, personally I was not prepared for what had just happened and it affected me emotionally. The intellectual versus the personal was like how someone once explained to me the difference between recession and depression. He said, "A recession is when your neighbor loses his job. A depression is when you lose yours." That incident and that anger was something I carried close to me for the next three years of my Air Force career.

My instructors were great. They treated me fairly and I met a lot of good people in school. However, when my schooling was over, I left Biloxi with a big chip on my shoulders. My next tour was in Duluth, Minnesota as a certified Surveillance Technician.

DULUTH, *Minnesota*

Duluth was a small town. If you were Black, it was even smaller. There weren't many points of interest for people of color. For entertainment, there was one nightclub downtown, The Rendezvous. This was a real dive with a bar, a pool table, juke box, and a hard wood dance floor with uneven boards. The air base didn't offer much either, there was one big recreation center with ping pong and pool tables. There were also some tables for playing games and several televisions throughout, those were the two major attractions on most weekends.

I spent twenty-five months at Duluth Air Base, a lot can and did happen within that time. I met a lot of good people; some became lifelong friends that I still stay in touch with. To one of them, I became Godfather to his beautiful daughter, Trinity.

I arrived at my new barracks about 7:00 p.m. Got to my assigned room and met my two roommates, Pee Wee from Dayton, Ohio and Montgomery from Tuscaloosa, Alabama. The accommodations were not what I expected, I was thinking that everyone would have their own room. Instead, I went from one roommate in technical school to now two.

I wasn't in the room for very long before some feathers got ruffled. Small talk led to me mentioning that I had a 9:00 a.m. meeting in the morning with the housing commander. I was told by Pee Wee not to set my alarm clock because it would bother Montgomery. Apparently, he had an internal alarm that woke him every morning at the same time and that mine would throw his off.

I had two problems with that, one, I did not know Montgomery and wasn't going to chance being late for my first meet and greet. Two, I had just come from a place that played games at my expense. I said as nice as I could that I was setting my alarm clock. Pee Wee thought it was funny and told Montgomery that there was a new Sheriff in town. Montgomery was not laughing. That was an awkward first meeting, but we all became good roommates and friends.

Now that I'm years removed from that environment, as I look back, several things stand out to me. The extra jobs I had on base for instance, when I spend too much time outside in the winter, my feet start to bother me, and I'm reminded of the job I had on base at the gas station. I was pumping gas one day and the temperature with the wind chill was 20 below zero. My feet have not been the same since. I also had a job cleaning a building at night. After four months I got fired, and that firing taught me a good life lesson. The job was rated to be completed in three hours, 7:00p.m. to 10:00p.m., five days a week, I got paid for three hours at the agreed upon hourly rate.

For the first month I worked hard stripping and waxing the floors and getting a good work routine. I had the floors in great shape. After that, the three-hour job only took me two. Late one night my boss came looking for me during my last hour of work. I was nowhere to be found. The next day he asked where I was.

I explained that I was done and went home and asked if there was a problem. He said, "The problem is that I'm paying you for three hours and you did not work three hours." I asked him if the place was clean. He replied, "Yes, but that's not the point, three hours means three hours." While I understood, I felt that having the place clean was more important. Agree or not, he was the boss.

As time went on, I would clean for two hours and goof off the last one. After two months of that I started leaving a little bit early, five minutes became ten, ten slowly stretched to twenty. My boss came in one night fifteen minutes before the end of my shift. I was not there. I got fired the next day. I learned a valuable lesson. If you own a business, you can set the rules. If you are working for someone, the boss sets the rules. If you don't agree with the rules, don't take the job. If you take the job, follow the rules.

Duluth provided a few more memorable firsts, the first and only time I conspired with someone to take money from a guy playing blackjack. We were using marked cards. Our plan was to teach him a lesson because he was always bragging about things, and we just didn't like him. Things were going our way for most of the night; we were up a couple hundred dollars. Then in the course of what seemed like a few minutes, things got ugly. My partner had been drinking all night and it was starting to affect his playing. This was not good because he was the house dealer. He's just about drunk, getting loud and careless. During this time, a friend came in and wanted a seat at the table.

While waiting for a seat, he noticed something was going on between me and my partner. He said, "Fred, why don't you show him your whole hand?" I played a few more hands and left the table. That night could easily have been two more firsts, the first time getting caught cheating at cards, and possibly the first time getting shot.

There were times I tried playing the unfaithful boyfriend. I met this girl downtown. On our second date, she started telling me that twins ran in her family, and it was something we would have to be aware of if we got married. That was the last time I saw her. A few months later, I met a young lady at a house party. She was a student at a local college. She organized a small party for our second date. She was bringing some of her girlfriends from school and I was bringing some guys from the base. The party was at a motel. She got a large room for the night, Pee Wee brought his boom box, and there was food and drinks.

About twenty minutes after everyone had arrived, there was a knock at the door. It was a guy from their college, she had also invited him. Ten minutes later, he sat on the edge of the bed and started crying. He had a room several doors down from ours. It turns out that he is gay and is having some boyfriend issues. All the girls walked him down to his room. After forty-five minutes had passed, Pee Wee says, "Fred, you need to go get your girl so we can get this party started." We all agreed, and we all were curious, so we went to go get her. I knock on the door, she opens it, and we see everyone is crying. I said something like you need to leave him with his problems and come let's party. I reached out and gently grabbed her arm.

The door is still open, the sidewalks had been plowed, and about three feet of snow is banked on one side. When I grabbed her arm, she pulled away and started swinging her arms fighting me. I'm backing up and by the time I get control of her hands, we're outside and I have her pinned against the snowbank. I told her that I don't fight girls but when I let you go, if you come at me again, you will be the exception.

I let her go. The fellas and I go back to the room, get the boom box, the food, the drinks, and head back to the base. On the way, we're all laughing at what was a crazy night. Then someone said, "That girl was trying to kick your ass," more laughing. By the time I got to the mess hall the next morning, the talk was that I got my ass whipped last night, that was good for some more weekend laughs.

That night was my wakeup call, I decided the girl I wanted was back in Ohio and that became my only pursuit from that day on.

First time freedom from home coupled with immaturity can be a dangerous combination. Youthful bad decisions can impact you well into your adult life, some from which you may never fully recover. Being young and acting dumb can be lethal, much like drinking and driving, sometimes you get away with it and sometimes you don't. While the results can vary, it is always dangerous.

I also remember getting into two fights on the base. The first fight happened in the barracks after an intramural basketball game. It was an on-base tournament, we had just lost, and we were eliminated. Later that night, two buddies and I were in the latrine getting ready to shower. We were laughing and talking about the events of the game. Suddenly, this tall White guy who lived across the hall comes in and tells us (not ask) to keep it down because he is working the midnight shift and needs his sleep. He then walks over to my friend, takes one end of the towel he has around his neck, flips it in his face, and said, "Do you understand?"

We were waiting for my friend to react, but he does nothing, he says nothing. The guy starts to walk back to his room. I looked at my friend, then at this guy and it felt like I was back in Mississippi again. I instantly went into my promise mode to not take crap from anybody, anymore. I grabbed the towel from around his neck, put it around mine, caught up to this guy, and dared him to flip it in my face. He went to reach for the towel, and it was on! We were fighting up and down the hall, knocking fire extinguishers off the walls, rolling on the floor, and basically trying to inflict pain on each other.

People came out of their rooms and broke the fight up, but the damage had been done. The airman in charge of night security heard the commotion and was now standing there with his clipboard. We got written up and both received an article 15 but no disciplinary action was imposed.

The second fight, believe it or not, happened because a guy I thought to be a friend would not let me use his car. That's right, fighting over his car, how crazy is that? I had gotten paid from one of my side jobs and wanted to go off base to cash the check. I found my friend in the dayroom; this was the central part of the floor that had chairs for watching T.V. and tables for board games and playing cards. He was there with four other people talking and watching television.

I asked him if I could use his car to cash my check, he had loaned it to me one other time and I had returned it with more gas than when I got it. For some reason he said, "No," with no explanation. While I didn't understand why, it was his car, and I turned and began to walk away.

As I'm leaving, I hear him say something that I didn't quite catch. However, when I turned around, he and the people he was with were laughing. I had that Mississippi feeling again, only this guy was Black, but to me it didn't matter because I was determined to take no crap from anybody, Black or White.

As I turned and started walking towards him, my Sharon-Line upbringing began to surface. You see, I developed a skill for cussing/using bad words. I learned this behavior at a young age hanging out at Baily Park. The adults played organized baseball there and man could they cuss. I fell in love with that way of communicating and got very good at it.

So now I'm walking towards him saying some things he probably didn't expect. He is a lifer doing his second hitch. I think he was about six years in and was a staff sergeant, I'm in my first year and virtually with no rank. He was five feet ten inches tall, two hundred plus pounds, and was not about to let me embarrass him in that setting. When I got to him he was on his feet, and it was on! We started knocking over chairs and tables which was making a lot of noise. People were trying to break us up.

This dayroom was directly above the one on the first floor where the airman for night security was stationed, he comes up with clipboard in hand. The guy I'm fighting sees him and stops his action. My back is to the door, so I don't see him at first. When he walks in, two people are trying to restrain me and I'm still trying to fight; not good. He writes us up and we must report to the commander in the morning.

The guy I was fighting goes in first and comes out smiling, not a good sign for me. The commander is Black, he begins reading the report to me. In the report, the airman wrote, "I could tell by the look in his eyes that he wanted to attack me too." What came next made me feel like I was in some new kind of Mississippi hell. Here is this Black commander reading this report from this White airman and reading it like it is gospel. He told me that this was my second fight within a three-month period and that it looked like I had anger issues. I thought to myself, yea, when certain issues come up, I get angry.

He went on to say that if anything like this happens again, I was going to jail. I may have had anger issues, but I wasn't stupid. That was my last fight on that base. This time I got an article 15 that came with some discipline. I had to go around the walls of a bay with a tool that held a single edge razor blade scraping wax off the floor from the baseboard out to about three inches. I'm scraping the wax off the floor thinking about that comment the airman made about the look in my eyes and what he thought. It made me think about a comedy routine I once heard, the comic was talking about this character named Dolomite. At one point he said, "Dolomite was so bad, he could look up a bull's ass and tell the price of butter." I said to myself, "This airman was a White Dolomite, looking into my eyes and reading my mind." This allowed me something to laugh at while others were probably laughing at me on my knees in this hall.

Here's another Duluth take away I've filed under lessons learned. It's Saturday, I'm at the Recreation Center on base. It was somewhere between five and six in the afternoon when this guy walked in. He was dressed to impress; this brother was too clean to sit down. I guess he was afraid he would break the creases in his pants or something. It was obvious he had spent a good part of the day getting ready.

Not long after he arrived, a guy walked over to him and asked for a cigarette. You could smell this fella from ten feet away. He had been playing ping pong for the last three hours. His shirt was soaked with wet and dry sweat. Back then, cigarettes at the BX were nineteen cents a pack. When I heard and saw the exchange between Cool Breeze and the Sweaty Airman, I told myself there must be a lesson here somewhere. I asked Cool Breeze if he had a date or perhaps was going downtown? He said, "No, I just decided to hang at the Rec Center for a while and I'm going back to my room." Here this guy spent all that prep time to impress someone that couldn't afford a pack of smokes. This was my takeaway, if you are going to impress someone other than yourself, make sure they are worth the effort.

There were many good things about working and living in Duluth, my Air Force job was easy, and I enjoyed it. I worked in a building we called The Block House, no windows, the walls were three feet thick, and fortified with something they wouldn't tell us. It was said that the building could take a direct hit from most bombs and remain standing. The area I worked in was called the dark room, the only light in the room came from small desk lights and the radar screens that were blinking every ten seconds pointing out any aircraft moving across the areas we were monitoring. We would work two hours on and two hours off during our eight-hour shift, it was a good job.

There were good times shared with friends like Jimmy Bell and Ronny Pasco, both from Cleveland Ohio, also Durrell Burden form Lima Ohio just to name a few. I

spent hours at the rec center talking smack with the fellas while sharing stories from home as we shot pool, sometimes for money other times just for fun.

There were many nights in the room listening to music on Pee Wee's boom box while we discussed sports, women, and contemplating what our futures might look like. Saturday nights at the Rendezvous Night Club downtown were always fun, drinking and laughing at too many airmen trying to pick up too few women, some got lucky, most didn't.

Another thing I can't forget is learning how to play the card game pinochle and doing it for hours with good friends. One of those friends was our landlord, he had a duplex. My wife and I lived upstairs, and they lived on the ground floor. We called him Johnson. He was a retired military man married to a pretty Japanese lady that spoke broken English named Junko. Johnson was the first and only person I ever knew that was a true chain smoker. He would light one cigarette with a match and all the others were lit with the one he was smoking. He had a lit cigarette all day and night.

My fondest memories of Duluth was bringing my wife to live with me off base and how excited we were when she got pregnant with our first child.

Twenty-five months in the books. Time to move on to my next and final adventure in the USAF.

SAGLEK BAY, *Labrador*

My last tour of duty was Saglek Bay, Labrador in Canada, this was a base identified as isolated/remote. It was out in the boonies, a detachment of Goose Bay, Labrador, and the only way in or out was by plane. You receive mail and fresh supplies twice a week, weather permitting. Though my life was a living hell from time to time, my surroundings were getting colder and colder.

When I was processing out of Duluth, the clerk smiled, looked at me and said, "Saglek, I heard there's a girl behind every tree up there." I later learned that there are no trees on Saglek, it's above the tree line, that wasn't a problem for me because I'm married now.

I was thinking that this could be my worst assignment because I would be isolated from the outside world or my best one because it would give me time to figure out who I was, who I was not, and what direction I wanted to take my life after the military. This actually developed into a good tour for me, I worked on my military career and there were times that I held down three part-time jobs. Stereo components were the latest big thing in music, the money from those extra jobs allowed me to come home with some of the nicest components on the market.

Four months into my one-year tour there, I was offered a three month early out; that means instead of twelve months there, I would only do nine. I turned it down because if you have less than six months left on your four-year commitment when you leave your current tour, the Air Force won't reassign you; your active Air Force career is over. Leaving Saglek three months early would have left me with eight months to serve, and I would get reassigned. I wanted this to be my last tour, I was ready to leave the military and go home for good.

During this tour, I was thankful to discover that I was really the same easy-going, fun-loving, hard-working person that first entered the Air Force. I was even more thankful to learn that I wasn't the rage filled, easy to anger, prejudice person into whom I had once morphed.

As far as my direction in civilian life, I knew that there was a job at Packard Electric in Warren, Ohio waiting for me. I knew that I was anxious to get home as a husband and new dad. Beyond that, I was confident that I could handle anything that came my way and go from there, military training and experience were the foundation for that confidence.

There were two clubs on base, The Officer's club where nobody hung out (because there were only three of them), the NCO club where everybody hung out (including the officers). The NCO club was fun, always something going on. It was a spacious room with a large bar, lots of tables and chairs, and an area to play darts. Though we were isolated, it wasn't a boring time for me. Everybody had their own room that was equipped with a speaker, a phone, the standard bed, closet, and a table. The rooms were small but nice.

The speaker was there because the base had a music and D.J. room. New music from every genre came in monthly. Anyone could be a D.J., you only needed to sign up for a block of time you wanted that day, I would do it from time to time as D.J. Green Eyes. I had a pair of glasses that had green tinted lenses.

The phones were for making calls back to the states, they were referred to as "Morale Calls." Typically, if you saw someone with a strange look on their face, you waited until they spoke to you, that look might have been the result of a call back home that netted bad news.

There was also a darkroom for developing pictures, there were several guys that had an interest in that. One day, one of those guys came into the office and asked if I would go into the operations room and have my picture taken; I agreed. I sat at the radar monitor with the commander standing over me and he took the shot. He asked me because the base was in the middle of a beard growing contest and I was one of the few that wasn't in the competition. What I didn't know was that this guy had authored an article about the base and submitted it to Look, Time, and Ebony magazines for publication. Ebony bought it because we had a Black commander, Major J. J. Kelly.

A couple of months later, I got a call about one o'clock in the morning from a hometown friend, Stanley McGaha, that was in the military stationed in California. He called because he had just read the article in Ebony and saw me sitting at the radar monitor and wondered if I was still at Saglek. That's how I found out I was in Ebony. There were guys taking pictures all the time, so you never knew what was going on. I called home to brag about my new celebrity and to suggest that they buy as many magazines as they could carry. Though life in Saglek was hard at times, I did have my fifteen minutes of fame. The Ebony issue was in October 1969. The article is titled, "*Master of Air Defence*M" pages 124 to 130. I'm on the front page, upper left corner.

Here's how Ebony described the base and some of the conditions; It is managed by a 150-man Air Force team led by Maj. J. J. Kelly. They call themselves "The Professionals." Saglek Bay, a 6,224-acre plot of strategic real estate located in northern Labrador. The command is perched atop a rocky, snow-encrusted cliff that soars 1,800 feet above the North Atlantic. The nearest settlement is the tiny Canadian town of Goose Bay, 375 miles to the south. It's a trying assignment, one which must be conducted under conditions of extreme isolation and extreme weather. The weather at Saglek Bay includes a nine-month winter with snow two hundred inches deep, temperatures 27 to 38 degrees below zero, and wind gusts as fierce as two hundred miles an hour. Ebony did a wonderful job with the article and showed good taste by including my picture.

Believe me when I tell you no one volunteers for this assignment, you just wake up one day with orders from the Air Force to go. That is not the day to go gambling because your luck just ran out. The running joke here was that this place was worse than being in jail because at least in jail you get visitors.

Once there was a production put on to welcome two new airmen to the base. There were many people involved but the commander was the star of the show.

They brought them to the NCO club when they arrived. The commander was unshaven with his uniform dirty and wrinkled. He maintained a look of desperation. The plan was for the commander to convince the airmen that a mutiny had taken place, and he needed their help to take control of the base again. It was hilarious.

One night I got into a poker game with the commander and a few other people. Everybody at the table liked to gamble except me, I was just looking for something to do. I learned a valuable lesson that night, "Scared money can't win!" Every time I considered calling or raising, I thought about how hard I had worked for my money and what I was saving it for, and it influenced my play all night. Gambling is a lot different when you are not cheating with marked cards. That night cured any gambling problems that might have been in my future.

I had many friends there but only two to which I was close, Glenn Barlow and Sergeant Mort. Glenn was six feet-four inches tall, about two hundred fifty pounds. He didn't have many friends on the base. He was from New Orleans, arrogant, loud, and at times obnoxious. With only one week left at Saglek for me, he and I started a mini riot.

The NCO club had a long-standing tradition of throwing people out in the snow, most of the time there would be six to eight feet of snow on the ground. Two people would grab a person, one would have the feet and the other would be behind grabbing under the armpits. The person would get carried to the side door, someone would open it, and the individual would go flying out! There was very minimal struggle because it was all in fun.

One night, Glenn asked me if I would help him throw this White guy out that was sitting at the bar facing out at the room. When I saw who it was, I said, "Yes!" Glenn was the only guy on base that was disliked more than him. We had never taken part in this ritual, never throwing someone out or being thrown out. It would usually happen after people got drunk; we never drank that much. So here we go, we're both committed now to doing this. There's just enough room between his chair and the bar for me to get in behind him, I'm in place and Glenn is standing in front of him. The guy is sitting with a drink in his hand. I reached and took his glasses off, turned and placed them on the bar countertop. When I started taking his glasses off, Glenn was reaching for his ankles. As I turned back around to get his arms, something happened that no one had seen before, this guy took his glass and smashed it into the side of Glenn's head!

The room went silent because everyone was looking at what we were about to do. Glenn goes down on one knee, takes a handkerchief out of his back pocket, and puts it to his face. When he pulled it away, it was covered with blood. No one in the club came to Glenn's aid and no one denounced the act, they were somewhere between shocked and happy. Glenn is still on one knee on the floor. This guy is now standing in silence over him. I looked at the blood, looked at this guy and said, "You really did this!" Before he could turn around, I hit him on the side of his face and knocked him down!

When I did that, it was like someone turned on the loud noise switch and all hell started breaking loose! Some guys grabbed Glenn, others were picking this guy up, and three other guys were shouting and dragging me out of the club to a lounge across the hall. They snatched me so hard I lost a shoe. These people are berating me for sucker punching this guy. Hitting Glenn was fair game I guess.

When Glenn got cleaned up, he found me and asked if I would help him find the guy that hit him. I said, "Yes," and we kicked in three doors to rooms we thought they might be hiding him in. We didn't find him. The night was finally over.

The next day was a little strange for me; no clip board reporting, no article 15, it was as though everybody wanted to erase that night and hope that nothing like that ever happens again. I was told that the guy I hit had blood coming out of his ear and that perhaps his ear drum was busted. It was too soon after the incident, I didn't care and was grateful that I was leaving for home in a couple of days.

GOING HOME; *Youngstown, Ohio*

I remember packing my duffel bags and preparing to make the rounds to say my goodbyes thinking, "This is the last time I'll have to deal with this! I'm finally going home for good!" I felt great about the decision I made to choose the four-year Air Force career rather than being drafted to a two-year military commitment with an almost certain one-year stint serving and fighting in Viet Nam.

I remember going in thinking about the four-year commitment I signed up for and comparing it to the four years of high school. Your first day of school as a freshman makes the vision of walking across the stage and receiving a diploma seem eons away. That high school experience helped me in the first few months because I knew that one day it would happen, now that day is clearly in view. I'm not only going home in a few days; I would be home. I say it that way because in my mind, I had been working my way home for almost four years now.

I had visualized the home coming celebration many times over the years. The type of celebration had changed over time, but it was always pictured as something I looked forward to. I remember my most recent vision being the plane landing and my wife holding our new baby boy, waiting to greet me at the end of the walkway in the airport. We would be laughing and hugging looking forward to starting this new chapter in our lives. However, that Norman Rockwell home coming was shattered for me with the culmination of events that happened a few months prior to me leaving Saglek.

You see, all those cheerful homecoming visions were quickly and painfully replaced with the reality of coming home to get a divorce. The uncertain start to my Air Force career has now shifted to an even more uncertain finish. I was transitioning from military to civilian life and very possibly from being married to a single divorcee with a child.

That NCO club melee, my last week at Saglek, gave me an opportunity to release some pent-up emotions and frustrations that had been brewing for a while; the last three weeks to be exact. You see, my friend Glenn was a big guy and didn't need me taking up for him. He was perfectly able and capable of fighting his own battles. The truth is, I had been wanting to hit something or someone since my last "morale call." These were the calls you used the phone in your room for to stay in touch with your loved ones back home. Most of my calls back home, on the weekend, were between midnight and 3:00 a.m. Ohio time. I found that to be the best time block because few people wanted it, which allowed me unlimited time to talk. That time was also good for my wife, and we treated it like a weekend date night.

During most of my time at Saglek, she was either pregnant or recovering from the birth of our child. However, now she's back at work and has a lot more options with how she could spend her weekends. My Saturday night call, ten weeks prior to leaving Saglek, was quite different from all the others. It's 2:15 in the a.m. and instead of the soft hello greeting from my wife, it was a sleepy but measured hello from my mother-in-law. I was incredibly surprised to hear her voice. I apologized for waking her and asked to speak to my wife. She slowly admitted that she wasn't at home. I asked if there was anything wrong? She said that nothing was wrong, my wife just went out for the night. I apologized again and wished her a good night.

In those days, Youngstown didn't offer much by way of late-night entertainment. There were a few bars and nightclubs and a couple of restaurants that stayed open late, late usually meant "Last call for alcohol" about 1:30 a.m. and locks on the doors at 2:00 a.m. When I hung up the phone from my mother-in-law, the clock said 2:20 their time, where the hell was my wife? I found that to be a reasonable question.

I called again that Sunday evening at about 8:00 p.m. My wife answered the phone. I cut straight to the point, "Where were you last night?" After a few laps of beating around the bush, it came down to her first night out since having the baby and she lost track of time. I've always considered myself a reasonable person, so it didn't take a lot of imagination to see and understand the picture she was painting. Her explanation was in apologetic tones and seemed sincere. I accepted her apology, but it came with conditions.

I explained my deep disappointment in clear and understandable terms. I pointed out that she was no longer representing herself in the streets as Miss. Sandra Lynn Henderson but as Mrs. Frederick H. Stringer, the mother of our son, and that I would not tolerate being disrespected. I said a few other things to encourage her and to let her know how proud of her I was for the way she was managing all the new things she was responsible for. However, I reemphasized the respect issue and that being in the streets until the wee hours of the morning was going to be very problematic for our marriage going forward. I asked if she had any questions or if there was anything additional she wanted to say. Her reply was, "No." We agreed to move forward.

The next five weekends were a mix of Friday and Saturday calls. Week six was a Saturday night call that started and ended with me talking to my mother-in-law again. This was not good because it was 2:35 a.m. (Sunday morning) and my wife was not home. I called Sunday evening for her explanation, and it was identical to the one she gave me six weeks prior; lost track of time. My response, however, was vastly different from the one six weeks earlier. I declared, in a very calm voice, that I would be coming home and filing for divorce. I let her know that one chance would not be rolling over to two.

When people do things and they are not sure of the response, then a conversation is warranted to make feelings and understandings clear. However, when people do things with a clear understanding of the response, it is reasonable to assume that the perpetrator has little or no respect for the victim. I may not have used the word divorce six weeks ago, but I know I used the term "problematic for our marriage if that situation presents itself again."

Now, with the goodbyes from Saglek behind me and a shaky future ahead of me, I'm flown to the base at Goose Bay, Labrador to start separation paperwork from the Air Force. I arrived Friday night and will be staying in temporary transit barracks for a few days. It's been four weeks since the divorce conversation with my wife, we had not spoken since. This could be viewed as a "cool down" period but I was as disappointed and angry on my first day at Goose as I was when divorce first came out of my mouth. We would have one more conversation before our eventual face-to-face meeting and that would be to pass along information to pick me up at the airport.

It's Saturday afternoon on my first full day at Goose. I slept in, cleaned up, and I'm now standing in the lobby at the main desk talking to the airman in charge of the barracks about life and the Air Force. His name was Mike. I asked how long he had been stationed there and explained that I'm headed home for good, I also asked what there was to do on base for the weekend. His response surprised me a little when he asked what did I have in mind. He said it like we were in New York City and the options were endless. Now granted, just about anything would beat where I had just come from, but I wasn't expecting as many options as his matter-of-fact response was suggesting.

I mentioned how long I had been at Saglek since my last visit home and that things were a little shaky on the home front. He asked if I was looking for a good place to eat, a nightclub with live entertainment, or just a bar that offered sandwiches where I could drink and eat without being bothered. The lobby wasn't busy, so we talked and laughed for about an hour. He was a nice young man with a bright future and seemed to welcome our conversation. I was getting hungry now and asked about lunch options. After settling on where to eat lunch, I inquired about the night club with the live band. That sounded like something fun to do and could take my mind off the serious matters bouncing around in my head, at least for a few hours. I decided to check it out.

We were parting company, me to lunch and him back to work behind the desk. I had taken a few steps away when he called me back with an option that changed the course of that night. Years after this night, I would ponder what category to file it under; fun, wild, stupid, careless, crazy, scary, a night to remember, or one with all my might to try and forget. He mentioned that he thought that I was a nice guy and asked if I wanted any company at the night club. He went on to say that he had a nice lady friend that was at the club most weekends and wanted him to be on the lookout for possible "Good-Guy" dates. Married or single didn't matter to her because she had recently divorced and was just looking to relax and have fun, nothing serious.

My initial mental response was, "No thanks," but then I thought about my situation back home and said "Sure, why not." I figured that I would soon be single, so I might as well get some practice in. Her name was Mary, a schoolteacher on base. He described her as part Eskimo, part European, nice body, five feet four inches, about 120 pounds, fun personality, a self-proclaimed nymphomaniac, and likes to drink top shelf whiskey. After that, he smiled and asked if I still wanted him to set up the date. He had a look on his face like, "last chance to run."

Nothing he said really bothered me because I wasn't thinking that far ahead, I just wanted a night to chill and if it rolled into something sexual, then so be it. When he used the word nymphomaniac, I took it to mean she enjoyed having sex and I did too so that wasn't a red flag for me. He made the call and told me she would be seated at the bar at 8:00 p.m. I said, "O.K.," and thanked him.

He said that he had a friend that would be on duty after his shift and that he would have him look out for me if we decided to come back to the barracks after the night club. He also showed me how to sneak Mary in the side door if needed. It turns out that you are not allowed to have company in the transit barracks. I started to feel my mood getting lighter and my Youngstown issues slowly shifting to the back of my mind; I'm looking forward to relaxing at the club.

It's 7:30 p.m., I'm dressed, leaving my room to catch the

shuttle to the night club. I walk in the club about 7:45 p.m. and someone fitting her description is already seated at the end of the bar. I walked straight towards her, and I'm pleasantly surprised at what I'm seeing. When Mike at the desk said his friend had a "fun personality," I took that as code for "she's not very pretty." She wasn't gorgeous, but I found her to be quite cute with her chubby cheeks. She had straight black hair, bedroom eyes, and a pretty smile showcasing white pearl-like teeth. I liked what I saw and asked if she was Mary. She said, "Yes and I presume you're Fred." I said, "Yes," reached for her hand and her drink and escorted her across the room to one of the empty booths along the wall and our date was officially started.

The club was sparsely populated because the night was young for a nightclub; the band wasn't scheduled to start until 9:30 p.m. Neither of us was hungry so we were content with ordering drinks and making "tell me about yourself talk" while we waited for the band to start. It's now a little after 10:00 p.m., the band is playing, the place is packed, we're enjoying each other's company when she grabs my hand and asks if I have anything to drink in my room. I let her know that I had several bottles of Crown Royal that would love to join our party.

With that, she smiled and led me out of the club to her car.

She had told me earlier that since her divorce, she had been living with her mother. She drove us back to the barracks and "plan B" at my place was now being activated. Back at the barracks, I go in the front door and have a few words with the airman on duty. I let Mary in the side door, and we are about to fast track the next phase of our evening.

There is nothing that says romance about this room except the light switch on the wall and the bed. The room had a small closet, a small chest of drawers, a small table with two chairs, and two small bedside tables, one had a lamp on it and yes, the lamp was small too. If you needed to use the restroom, you had to leave the room, this was a typical barracks with the central urinals, showers, sinks, and mirrors located in the middle of the hall which was two doors down from my room.

I went to get cups and ice. When I returned, she was standing at the table with her hand on the bottle of Crown Royal. The room was much different than when I left, the ceiling light was off and the lamp on the side table was on. She also looked much different, she was wearing nothing but her bikini panties and that pretty, now looking like a million-dollar smile. I walked in the room, took a quick look around and was out of my clothes like some kind of magic trick; like she had said "ABRACADABRA," snapped her fingers, and behold all my clothes disappeared.

I poured us both a drink and pulled our bodies together briefly. She reached for her drink, and I reached for her breast. She put her drink back on the table and put her hand on top of my hand that was on her breast. She pulled my hand away and placed it inside her panties. Whatever conversation that was going on at that time stopped, her body started doing all the talking for both of us. It was screaming, "I'm moist and I am ready." My body heard those cries and responded in-kind. She opened her purse to reveal a variety of condoms, got me suited up, and for the next however long it lasted, nobody gave a second thought about those drinks. It was on!

It had been months since I had felt the warmth of another body next to mine and the sensation was more than inviting, it was almost overwhelming. I think in those first few minutes, I had forgotten how to even spell Youngstown. At that time, there were no negative thoughts in the room for me at all. However, what I didn't know was that the night was incredibly young and that "good now" doesn't always translate into "good later."

At some point, round one was over for me, it wasn't quick, but it was over. I got up and brought her drink over to her while I went to freshen up. When I came back, I grabbed my drink, lit a cigarette, and sat up in bed with her. I knew that I had gotten more out of that round than she did, like I said, it had been a while for me. After a minute or two, she looked over at me and said, "It's taking you a long time to smoke that cigarette." I knew what that meant, she was ready. She was treating what just happened like foreplay, now she wanted her fireworks and that was all right with me. It was on to round two!

This time I thought that I had brought home the bacon. Now I quit before she did but just barely. When I stopped, for obvious reasons, she stopped and there was plenty of wet evidence that she was not having a bad night. I'm thinking that I well represented the Sharon Line, the state of Ohio, and quite possibly the entire Brotherhood nation. I went to freshen up saying to myself, "I bet she'll let me smoke a cigarette now." I was also thinking that if the night was over, it would be a good thing, I was worn out!

The night had already exceeded my expectations. I'm thinking about taking her to her car and me getting some sleep, but she was thinking about making it clear to me that she was representing the Nymphomaniac nation. Mary's real life, emotional, Three-D definition of nymphomania was slowly but surely replacing the intellectual one I had pictured somewhere within the pages of Webster's Dictionary; the one that I thought would be fun to experience someday. However, she was about to teach me the difference between what's real and what's imagined. The night was far from over and I was not in shape for what was looking like a night of marathon sex, like I said, it had been a while.

The night is slowly slipping away and there is no verbal conversation in the room. I'm sitting on the edge of my side of the bed smoking a cigarette. She is sitting up against the head-board on her side drinking, but her eyes are half closed. I'm hoping she'll finish her drink, drift off to sleep and when she wakes, I take her back to get her car. However, that was my wish only, hers was quite different. The course of events that happened next are some of the things I remember most when-ever I reflect on that evening, she could tell that my interest in her smoking hot body was not the same as it was when we first flashed skin. She finished her drink and proceeded to do something to get me back in the mood. I'm still sitting on my side of the bed smoking; my head is down looking at the floor. She gets up, walks around the bed, and is standing in front of me. Her skin is glistening from the glow of the lamp on her side table.

She then takes the cigarette out of my hand and puts it out in the ash tray on my side table. I'm still mostly looking down at the floor when she takes my chin in her hand and pulls my head up to where we are looking into each other's eyes. She breaks her stare, glances down at my manhood, and sees no reaction to her presence. That's when she started working her magic towards round three.

She knew I had a strong interest in her lovely breasts, but she kept them off limits to me for most of the night. Now she is not only bringing them into play, they are her play. She takes both of my hands and brings them up to caress them, then she removes my hands, grabs her breasts, and begins to move her nipples very slowly across my lips creating a sensation of kissing and licking at the same time. My hands are on her hips. Now, there is positive movement below, so a reluctant and somewhat painful round three is about to begin.

At some point during this session, a maneuver was made, and she is now on top, straddling my waist, sitting up facing me. We had settled into a nice back and forth groove with my hands on her hips and hers on my chest. Her vocals were a low controlled moan. Then, in an instance, as though someone had turned on a switch, everything got amped up. Her moans have now turned into muffled screams, I say muffled because an effort was made all night to keep the noise to a minimum to avoid detection from neighbors.

The easy back and forth has totally left the room, she is now riding my already sore hips like you would see a cowboy riding a bucking bronc in a rodeo; the only thing missing was a twirling hand in the air. This catches me off guard and now we are no longer in sync. I may have started this fire inside her but now she is fanning the flames mostly on her own, Mary is doing Mary.

This went on for what seemed like hours, though for sure, it was nowhere near that, it was just so painful, it felt like a long time. It got so bad; at one point I faked an orgasm trying to bring things to an end. My fake gratification had no impact on her, whatever world she was in, continued uninterrupted.

Now she's getting louder. Her twerking and gyrating has gotten more intense, and her hands are no longer on my chest. Now she's sitting straight up on my hips with both hands cupping and fondling her breasts while alternating looks up at the ceiling and back down at me. Her vocals have gone from screams to a constant broken record of "Oh, you are so much man." I did not take comfort in that praise because at some point during all that, my manhood had turned into a wet noodle lying somewhere limp between my thighs and she continues to scream to the world about how much man I am.

At this point, I'm just lying there watching the Mary show while my mind begins to wonder. My first thought was that maybe I don't like sex as much as I thought I did. That was followed by, "Could I be gay?" That thought had a short life. My next question to myself was a game changer, "Could this be some new kind of conspiracy to commit murder, death by sex?" I thought about how easy everything fell into place and the fact that I really didn't know any of the players. As crazy as that was sounding even to me, whatever fun that might have been remaining in the bed, just got up and left the room. My conspiracy theory is really bringing this night to an end for me. I felt like I was wide awake in the middle of a nightmare.

She finally let out one last loud vocal and collapsed face first onto my chest. She has either had one of those multiple orgasms I had heard about, or this chick has just peed on me. She is lying on me and her whole body is trembling. I first think that this is a good thing but because my current mental condition is in over-drive, I begin to wonder, could this be the beginning of her having a seizure? A few minutes later, she is still shaking and then starts to cry. I can feel her tears against my skin. Not one of those twist your face up, boohoo cries, just a sniffle or two but her tears are flowing.

They could be tears of joy, or perhaps wishing that this night should have been shared with her X; I don't know. I didn't ask, and she made no effort to explain those emotions. I thought that if I have to go get some help for her, someone might want to throw me in jail for something; if for nothing more than her tears. She's almost White, I'm very Black and we all know how that can play out. Mary stops trembling, stops crying, looks at me, smiles, and gives me our first and last kiss of the night. She is ready to go home and I'm ready to take her to her car. The night is finally over, nobody's sick, nobody has to go to jail, and oh let's not forget, I'm still alive!

I walk her back to her car. We give each other a long hug that we both understood to mean, thanks for the night and that we'll probably never see each other again. Back inside, I clean the room, got fresh sheets, took a welcomed shower, and went to bed thinking tomorrow is another day.

I woke up Sunday afternoon and couldn't escape thinking about the reality waiting on me. I now have a broken heart, a sore you-know-what, and my head is filled with more questions than answers. Part of my reality check is that in about forty-eight hours, I'll be in Ohio, getting off a plane and greeting people I call my family with the real threat of divorce looming.

The remaining time I had left at the Goose was spent in isolation just thinking about things, mostly family stuff. I also thought about that last week at Saglek and concluded that it was a bad footnote to what was an outstanding tour for me. With that being said, that incident the last week taught me a valuable life lesson, although I had worked hard at turning my career around and moving towards a positive attitude, looking back at the events of that night in the NCO club, made it extremely clear that I still had some growing up to do. I realized that I didn't totally grow up in the Air Force; I merely did some growing. I discovered that self-improvement is not a destination, it's a process. You don't wake up one day and suddenly find that you have arrived.

When you're young and angry, sometimes you don't make the best decisions. Saturday night should not have happened, but it did. Saturday night didn't change anything that happened back in Ohio weeks ago, Saturday night had not softened my heart on plans for a divorce.

I'm ready to go home but I'm not sure I'm ready to deal with whatever was coming next. My Air Force career is just about over, and my uncertain civilian life was about to begin again. Looking back at that specific time in my life, I wish that I had been deeper in my faith because my situation called for some serious prayer, and I was empty. I once heard an Air Force veteran sum up his career this way, "I wouldn't go back for a million dollars, but I wouldn't trade the experience for two million." I can't say that I agree with those dollar amounts, but I do with the point being made.

CHAPTER 5

-HOW A MENTOR CHANGED MY LIFE

Are you a mentor or a mentee?

I think that most people of adult age would have to admit the world we live in and our ability to navigate through it can be profoundly serious, complicated, and difficult at times; this includes relationships, financing a lifestyle, and staying sane, just to name a few. When we are born, we're thrust into what I call the game of life. Approaching life as a game was extremely helpful to me because I understood the basic concepts of playing games, this helped me to simplify things. Games have rules, the rules are not there to help you but rather to keep you in-line and to level the playing field, on paper that means to make it fair for all the players.

Another basic concept of the game approach is understanding that there are winners and losers, if you choose to be on the winning side of things, then the first thing you need to do is learn the rules of whatever situation you might find yourself in. Now, if the rules are not there to help you win then how do you get to a place of a winning advantage?

There are many ways to gain an advantage, generally, when you say that, the first thing that comes to mind is money. While money can be a difference maker in the game of life, it can also be as much a hindrance as help. Some rich people are as miserable as people who don't have two nickels to rub together.

Sporting games come with rules, but they also come with coaches and trainers. While the rules are there to level the playing fields, the coaches and trainers are there to unlevel them, they are there to give their players and team an advantage. In the game of life, I call the coaches and trainers mentors. As we live our lives, we are constantly surrounded and impacted by mentors. Also, as we experience life, we ourselves are bouncing between being a mentor and mentee.

I have taken part in some mentoring programs that were very formal. They spelled out the process, intention, stated short and long-term goals for both the mentor and the mentee. It was also understood as to who the mentor and the mentee were. I suggest that informal mentoring is more prevalent because it goes on around us constantly, it's just not labeled. We are watching and learning from other people and they watch and learn from us. Understanding this concept has the ability to make huge impacts on us and the people we interact with.

In this chapter, I will share three specific concepts I uncovered that changed my life for the better. They are things that have become pillars in my life that came from a mentor who will probably never know that he gifted them to me. With that being said, I will be forever grateful to him and his gifts.

As an adult, I experienced two separate sets of circumstances that caused me to make changes in my Christian walk. It drove me to change my church home both times. If you are raised in a church environment, as a child, you go where your parents either tell you to go or take you. When you become an adult, you make those decisions, and you have to deal with the benefits or consequences.

I loved both of the churches I finally left and left for similar reasons. The second was a church that I was a member of for about 29 years. I considered myself part of the leadership there and it was an extremely difficult decision to leave. However, I landed at the church I currently attend, and everything happens for a reason. I talk about those two departures in the chapter on "**Leadership**."

This was kind of a long introduction to get to what I really want to cover in this chapter. I find that sometimes you have to trace your steps to remind yourself and better understand how you landed in the situation you might find yourself in.

After attending my new and current church for several months, the senior pastor invited me to attend an eight-week class on discipleship that he taught. I accepted the invitation and looked forward to the experience. We met every Wednesday evening in his office. The class was very structured with written homework assignments to be completed each week. He would do this twice a year and personally hand pick and invite sixteen men from the church each time. Each of the eight weeks had a different subject, task, and goal. However, the paperwork we received the first day spelled out a task that was personal and would be addressed at the end of each class over the course of the eight-week period.

Thirty minutes would be saved at the end of each class and two people would give presentations on this homework; each was given fifteen minutes. The task seemed straight-forward and somewhat simple but proved to be anything but. This was the assignment; "name three places, three events, and three people that had the greatest impact on your life." The only rule was that one of your persons could not be Jesus.

Part of the goal for the class was to give each of us an opportunity to meet, interact, and possibly build bonds with fifteen men from the church. The pastor explained why the class was for men only. At one time, the class rotated between husbands and wives and just men. Over time he realized that the men opened up more when the room was full of men only.

The presentations were all over the place, some brought the drama and heartbreak that was worthy of a Hollywood film. Seemed like every week, at least one presenter would become overwhelmed with emotion to the point of tears. Some talked about events that hurt so deeply they had never mentioned it until the night they presented. It seemed easy to relate and attach emotionally because as men, we understood the difficulty in opening up to raw, real emotions.

It's now the seventh week and it's my turn to share. I was glad that it took that long because I changed some of my choices several times. I took the assignment to heart and wanted to be as honest as I could, looking over my lifetime and choosing only three for each category proved to be quite challenging. The one I struggled with the most was "three people" that had the greatest impact on my now senior life. One of the three people that made my final cut was someone that no one in my family or circle of friends had ever heard of until recently because I had never mentioned him by name. A second was a family member of my first wife and would probably shock everybody to know that he made my list. I talk about him in the chapter "**Family**."

Back to the mystery person that no one ever knew existed in my life. In the chapter "**Growing up in the USAF**," I talk about some events and adventures that happened during that period of my life. A lot of what I shared was not good for me. However, whenever I look back on my time in the Air Force and reflect on the impact this person had on my life, two things are clear. First, he offset the negative things and made the entire experience seem worthwhile. Second, when I considered the instructions on that homework assignment, "greatest impact on my life," he deserved to be one of my three choices.

My Air Force tenure allowed me to cross paths with a lot of people, some were real characters. However, there was one that truly stood out to me because he changed my approach to living life. I respectfully refer to him as one of my most significant mentors. The definition of mentor is "*a person looked upon for wise advice and guidance.*" This person didn't have the title of mentor in my life, his title was my boss. It wasn't until he left, and I started remembering and recording our time together that I realized how much he had impacted me.

He was a Master Sergeant that was over my unit at Saglek Bay, my last assignment before leaving the Air Force. I reported to him and recognized over time he was the best boss

I ever had. We became fast friends. I also recognized after a brief period of time; he was different. There was something that made him stand out. We called him Sergeant Mort or just Mort, he didn't care.

Saglek Bay was an isolated, remote twelve-month tour of duty. People came at various times which meant that assignments would have to be rearranged as people left. I was working on the "radar floor" when Mort's office manager's tour was up. He asked if I would consider taking his place to manage the office. I accepted the offer and began to work side by side with him 8 hours a day, 5 days-a-week. Best job ever!

About four months later, it was time for Mort to leave and go to his next assignment. It was always a joy working and being around him. His personality gave him a presence that was father-like or grandfather-like, or your favorite uncle, your best friend, or the brother you admired and looked up to. When he was talking with you, he was also listening to you.

His physical appearance had extraordinarily little bearing as to who he was. He always looked like a professional soldier, clean and polished but at the same time, very ordinary. In a less than crowded room, you would never single him out to be the most likely to succeed at any subject you might pick. He was average height, about 5 feet, 9 inches, average looking, balding, with Basset Hound like eyes, and a digit missing from the middle finger on his left hand. The one thing that was distinctive about him was the ready smile he would always have for you that never seemed fake.

The day has come, the entire base has gathered to send him off. We're smiling and wishing him well but behind the façade, most of us were sad to see him go. A silence quickly came over the cheering crowd as his plane taxied and took off. Mort was gone; there was no one that could really take his place.

On what seemed to be a long walk back, another friend that had the same rank as Mort came along side me and said something that became the catalyst that helped me to become the person I am today. It started with a question he asked me, "Everybody is making a big deal over Mort, were you ever in his room?"

I said, "No, I never had a reason to go to his room."

He then said, "Well, I did." He had an entire bookcase filled with books on subjects like; how to influence people, how to handle people with different personalities, how to make a difference in people's lives, and what to do when things go wrong in your life. He also mentioned other topics, but his point was that Mort's entire personality and persona was learned behavior. He stated that everything about him was learned by reading and studying books.

It was at that moment I learned that he was jealous of Mort. This guy was Black, and did I forget to mention, Mort was White. While they both had the same rank, he was not looked upon or treated like Mort. While his comments were meant to disparage Mort, it had a uniquely different impact on me. It also didn't change the way I felt about Sergeant Mort. I was never jealous of Mort, but I did admire, like, and respected him a great deal. I liked how he controlled his space and how people reacted to him. He made me want to be a better man. What that Master Sergeant unwittingly did was plant a seed in my mind that made me think that I too could possibly acquire some of those same qualities I loved about Mort. So, I started to orchestrate a plan to make it happen. If only in part, what the Sergeant had said about Mort was true and he morphed into the person he was by studying books, my plan was going to be to study Mort.

I had a little less than four months left in the Air Force. I started carrying a pad and pen with me everywhere I went. I tried to recall and record as much as I could about everything Mort. The different situations that came up in the office, how he talked to people that came in the office and in social settings, how he responded to people when they sought his advice, how he acted when things did or didn't go according to plans and anything else I could think of.

When I had reached the end of my time at Saglek, my task was complete. After studying my copious notes, I came up with three specific things that I felt represented the core of Sergeant Mort's success. I labeled these character traits as **"BUTTONS," "ACHILLES HEELS,"** and **"SEPARATION."** I have applied these three to my life from the time I left the Air Force to this very day. I have personal testimonies as to how these have impacted my life in incredibly positive ways. I am convinced that if properly understood and applied, anyone can experience quality of life improvements also. Here's how they work.

Matthew 7: 13 & 14 (NIV), *"Enter through the narrow gate. For wide is the gate and broad is the road that leads to destruction, and many enter through it. But small is the gate and narrow the road that leads to life and only a few find it."* Often time when I reflect on these three lifestyle directions, I'm reminded of those Bible verses. I say that because **"Buttons," "Achilles Heels,"** and **"Separation"** goes against the grain of how the average person approaches life; they choose to "go through the wide gate."

Once you understand these three concepts, you begin to understand why Mort was such a standout. He chose the "narrow gate," the one that few choose. That path is harder to find and the average person or the majority of people, don't even know to look for it. That path requires a greater effort to stay on it. However, I believe that finding ways to navigate it will yield positive results in a person's life.

We are emotionally attached to the people in our lives at diverse levels, some we like, some we love, some we don't like, and some we might actually hate. Then there are other categories we label people with; some we are forced to spend time with, perhaps job related, some we don't want to be around, some we enjoy spending time with. Then there are people we do not want to disappoint; these are the ones that are special in our lives.

The difference between some of these categories are subtle and objective, it really depends on the value you place on the word or category. For me, being a person in someone's life they don't want to disappoint is truly special. I place a high value on that. It's like the difference people often place on the value of a diamond wedding ring, there is the price tag and then there is the emotional. To someone that has had a wonderful marriage, that ring reflects the memories associated with the marriage which makes the ring priceless. It's really the memories that are priceless and can't be replaced which gives the ring the higher value than the price tag. Positive memories are the key to how you get to that status in a person's life; they don't want to disappoint you.

I believe that when you are around people that enjoy your company and you enjoy theirs, your life feels easier and more fulfilling. It creates a certain comfort level within this stress-filled world we live in that is always welcomed. That feeling is what I always felt whenever I was around Mort. I always knew that I reported to him, but it seldom felt like a boss-subordinate environment. He created space around himself that was comfortable and uplifting. He made you feel safe, like you could count on him to always have your back.

BUTTONS

Most people associate the term *"Pushing someone's buttons"* with something negative because that is what the majority of society does; "the wide gate." However, the buttons I'm referring to is just the opposite. My buttons are a mindset way of living. A way, for the most part, which yields positive results.

When that sergeant told me about Mort's book collection, I imagined that some of the charisma he generated might have come from those studies. It really didn't matter to me where it came from because to me it felt real. The feeling was so special, it always made him stand out no matter how crowded the room. One of the things I was looking for, as I studied Mort for those months, was how he was able to create that comfort zone and do it in a way that looked easy and natural for him. When I finally came up with what I thought he was doing and how he was doing it, I labeled it "**Buttons**."

What he was doing was not complicated at all, he was simply creating memories that were attached to emotional buttons that he could push to activate anytime he needed or wanted to. I see buttons as a currency of positive emotions or feelings. It's kind of like depositing money in the bank that you can later draw out to speak to your future needs and wants. Once I determined what he was doing, I needed to figure out the "how."

The "how" proved to be relatively uncomplicated as well, he made you feel like you were special to him. He got personal with you. He made you feel that you were better than you thought you were. Mort got back to human behavior 101; treat people like you want to be treated. His buttons were random acts of kindness and unexpected blessings with purpose.

Society has a way of beating you down over time. Sometimes the daily grind has a way of making you question certain things about yourself; occasionally even questioning your own self-worth. Life is simply challenging sometimes, so, imagine you meet someone that begins to pay you some attention and begins to build your self-worth. That makes you feel that you are not just special but special to them, most people would cherish those feelings and the relationship. Most people would take on the challenge of trying to prove that this person was right about them; yes, I am special, and most people would not want to disappoint this person.

When you reach that status of being "someone they don't want to disappoint," you now have earned buttons to push in this person's life. The fact that most people don't look for opportunities to lift others up is exactly why and how buttons work. When you go out of your way to make people feel special and show kindness in todays' world, you stand out and people cherish those moments. At first glance, you might see this as a form or type of manipulation. My response to that would be yes, there is some manipulation involved with my concept of "**buttons**." Truth is, we are constantly exposed to varying degrees and types of manipulations.

Either we are doing it to someone, or we are having it done to us, we're trying to get someone to see things our way or perhaps move them to the left or right on a point they are dogmatic about. How about media manipulation; television commercials, billboards, ads in newspapers, and magazines. Our world today is a non-stop smorgasbord of manipulation attempts. I don't have a problem with any manipulation you might want to assign to these "**buttons**." The reason being, I know the intent for which it is designed, the purpose is to engage and promote positive emotional feelings and memories.

Personal, one-sided manipulation that only benefits the ma-
nipulator is not what these buttons are about. That type of person is easy to spot, and most efforts are rejected. They are like
the playground bully. They will smile in your face in an effort
to get what they want, when the fake smile doesn't work, their
next move is to resort to who they are, and the bully comes
out. This can lead to an emotional event also, but it will mostly be negative. My button manipulation is mutually beneficial
and intended to help create and grow positive, healthy relationships.

There can be other people in our lives that we don't want to
disappoint but it comes from a different source, it's a negative
source of power or fear. Someone like our bosses, we don't
want to disappoint them for financial reasons, or perhaps
someone we are afraid of because of what they might physically do to us. They also have buttons to push, however, those
buttons and the possible end results are the total opposite of
the ones I'm promoting from my study of Mort.

You benefit most from the knowledge of buttons when you
find yourself in a leadership position. Don't be confused by
the term leadership position, don't tell yourself things like;
I'm not a supervisor or no one's reporting to me, or I'm not
a business owner. You're thinking too big. While those are

obvious positions of power, leadership opportunities are presenting themselves all the time.

How about in an organization you might belong to, have you ever been asked to head up some special committee? How about at church, there are wall-to-wall opportunities there because it's mostly a volunteer run system, Trustee Board, Usher Board, leaders of the choirs, and so on. Let's not forget all the celebratory functions that need someone to head those committees. How about in our home? Most parents are or should be the leaders in those environments. When you find yourself in one of those leadership positions that are tied to time sensitive goals, "buttons" can play a critical role. In situations like that, you need people on your team that you can count on, people that don't want to disappoint you.

I was a supervisor in engineering at the job I retired from. I was responsible for the design, build and debug of equipment called Assembly Dies. These dies are used to put metal clips on wires that are used to build wiring harnesses for the automobile industry. The dies were shipped to many locations around the world. These wiring harnesses were tied to start dates to build the various cars. This made everything in that process very time sensitive; the design of the components of the dies, the die builds, the harness builds, and instillations that needed to be in the cars to meet their delivery dates to the various car dealership showrooms. As you can see, there were a lot of moving parts that were all sequentially tied to one line start date at some car assembly plant.

One of my constantly reoccurring problems was that there were some components that went into my dies for which I was not responsible. They were designed and tested based on the type of metal clip for the type of wiring harness, this involved two other engineering departments that were out of my control. The real problem was that often times, there were revisions within that process that ate up time that could seriously impact the delivery of my dies. While the revisions drove change, the thing that didn't change was the line start date at the car assembly plants.

Part of my team was located in one of my colleague's work areas. One of the things that is common in most work plants is something we call scheduled break times; it would be a time of about fifteen minutes for people to take a break from work. From time to time, this colleague would come to my office to inform me that some of my guys were taking advantage of me by breaking longer than the scheduled time. It would be mentioned that if I pushed harder, I could get more out of them.

I'm sharing this story to show one example of how "**buttons**" can be mutually beneficial to both parties involved. I would let my guys know that I knew that they were occasionally abusing the break time and goofing off sometimes when they should be working. For the few times this happened, we would talk it through with me reminding them what they were there to do but I never blew it up to make a big deal of it. I never got the impression that my guys though that I was soft but more that I was a decent, caring, and understanding boss.

Here's the other side of this scenario, I knew that there would be times when I would need these guys to go the extra mile for me to meet some of our delivery date deadlines. You might say that I let some things slide occasionally and in return my guys didn't let me or the team down in those critical times; **"buttons"** on full display. When you always play strictly by the rules, don't be surprised when they are thrown back in your face. That can be extremely costly when you find yourself in a time of needing someone to go out of their way for you.

In my case, there were times when I would have a deadline delivery in jeopardy. In those times, I might need these guys to work through not just their fifteen-minute break but possibly lunch also. That request might be met with resistance if the work atmosphere was always run "strictly by the rules, no exceptions." Sometimes a little give and take can make an enormous difference.

I am not suggesting to break the rules or laws to gain favor with someone or some group, those are put in place to be followed and enforced. There are some protocols however, that have some flexibility built in. What I am suggesting is that when you have access to flexible situations, don't always take; give a little when possible.

In most leadership/boss scenarios, it's typical for the people under them to look for ways and go out of their way to gain favor with the leader. This is true because most people think that the boss wants to be treated like they are the boss. However, this button concept is just the opposite; "the narrow gate." Imagine this, when you find yourself in a leadership role, you go out of your way to reach out to gain favor with the people on your team. Most team members are not used to experiencing that approach and will see something different and refreshing with your leadership style. That difference could make a significant difference in how they feel and react to you, this type of behavior creates button possibilities.

While working in the office with Mort, he wrote a letter recommending me for "Airman of the month." I won that honor, and it later rolled into "Airman of the quarter" with a write-up of me in a national Air Force publication. I didn't know he was writing that letter until after he had submitted it. He made me feel special. He let me know that I was special to him. Do you think he earned any buttons with me? You bet he did!

You're the leader, a member of your team has a doctor's appointment and needs to leave early; you show concern and let them go. That's a button opportunity. A team member has ongoing family or health issues; you show concern and be as accommodating as you can. When most people are treated humanely with common courtesies, they are grateful, and those memories are held close and not soon forgotten. Right, buttons in play.

I mentioned earlier that my current pastor picked me as one of the sixteen men to participate in his special discipleship class. Later that year, he showed a lot of interest in my grandson's high school football team for which he was playing. Most of the time Sebastian, my grandson and I would attend church together. The Pastor would always greet us in the lobby and ask how things were going with me and at Sebastian's school.

One Sunday we met in the lobby, and he informed us that he had looked on-line and had gotten the playing schedule for Sebastian's football team. He then announced that he would like to attend one of the games with me. He just needed to check his schedule to see what Friday night might work best. He called me two weeks later on a Wednesday, to see if that Friday would be good for him to attend the game with me. He also asked if it would be O.K. if he brought the young man that is his "Little Brother" in a "Big Brother" program he was part of.

That Friday was a home game for Sebastian and happened to be against the school the Pastor graduated from. Now this is what I knew, this church is one of the largest in the area and are mostly White, so is the Pastor. There are three weekly services: 5:00 p.m. on Saturday, 9:00 a.m. and 10:45 a.m. on Sunday. The church had added 1,200 new members within the past twelve months. The Pastor was remarkably busy and active in all phases of the church. He could have spent a Friday night with any of the many members at the church and he chose me. He showed me two acts of kindness: inviting me to his class and going to the game with me. This made me feel special and let me know that I was special to him.

This is how I reacted for the Friday night game, I went to Dick's, a sporting goods store and purchased special cushions for him and his little brother to sit on. I took my insulated, over-sized lunch box and filled it with all sorts of snacks and drinks for them. I purchased reserved seating tickets and left them at the "will call" for them. We had a wonderful time at the game. I also got Sebastian's mom, my daughter a reserved seat ticket and we all had an incredibly special night at the game. The only thing that went off script was the Pastor's team winning; just kidding, kind of.

For the two and a-half years I had gone to Sebastian's games and the year and a-half that followed, I had never sat in the reserved seating section, nor had I ever brought snacks to a game. That was the first and only time that happened, I reacted the way I did because I wanted to make sure that the Pastor and his friend had an enjoyable Friday night. I did not want to disappoint him. You see, the Pastor had been building positive memories with me. These memories are the buttons that I'm talking about, it didn't matter if it was intentional or if it just happened. Those buttons put him in a category of someone I did not want to disappoint.

The truth is that button opportunities happen all the time. One of the keys is to not just wait for one but rather go out of your way to create some button memories. The more you understand this concept, the more you begin to recognize an opportunity when it presents itself. Equally important is understanding that the foundation "**BUTTONS**" it is built on is simply treating people like you would want to be treated.

ACHILLES HEELS

In Greek mythology, Achilles was an almost invulnerable hero. According to one version of the legion, Achilles' mother Thetis, held him by his heels and dipped him into the river Styx. This river was believed to be magical and to connect the earth to the underworld. She did this to render him invulnerable. She immersed every part of him except the heels she was holding him by. His story goes on to record that during a battle, he was struck by an arrow in his heel which was the cause of his death. That heel was his vulnerable point, his weakness. Achilles' vulnerable point was legendary; ours not so much but can be just as deadly. The ones we have can also kill, but the power it mostly possesses is destroying our relationships.

In my study of Mort, as I poured through my notes, one thing started to crystallize, Mort's relationships. In some of the situations I recalled, Mort was the bad guy. There were times in the office when he dispensed some harsh reality to some people that had screwed-up. Then, there were other times I saw and heard him play hardball with people and thought that he had stepped on someone's feelings harder than he needed to.

One day I questioned him about one of those encounters. I wanted to know why he was so hard on the guy, it happened in a social setting, the NCO Club, not the office. The club was fairly crowded, and I thought the guy would have been embarrassed by what he had said to him. Mort looked at me and laughed. He told me that what he had said meant nothing to this guy. He then went on to say that if he had said some other things to him, the situation would have been much different with a much worse outcome. He explained that he was probably pissed at him but in a day or two, they would be buying each other drinks again. And as I recalled, he was right. It wasn't long before they were laughing and drinking with each other again.

My review and take-away was several things, one was that the two of them were friends. Another was that Mort really knew his friend and what not to say. Lastly, knowing what not to say and not saying it meant that Mort wanted to preserve the relationship. My study made it clear to me that Mort put a high value on personal relationships. I concluded that this was one of the things that allowed him to stand out. It also showed me that how you treat someone reflects how you feel about them. Mort knew not to take relationships for granted and that they are to be handled with special care. It was like he understood the human nature of things when it comes to interacting with people.

After I understood how he handled relationships and the advantage it gave him, I labeled it "**ACHILLES HEELS**." His attitude and approach to safeguarding his friendships takes me back to the Bible verse that speaks to the "small gate" and the "narrow road."

We all have family and friends that we know very well. We know what makes them tick, what turns them on and off and most importantly, what would hurt them very deeply. The use of that knowledge is at the core of "**Achilles Heels**."

Here is a typical scenario when two people are arguing, if the situation gets heated and one person says something hurtful, the other one will retaliate with words that will probably be just as, if not more hurtful. Now, if this is between two individuals that don't really care about each other or the relationship, then the hurtful words probably won't matter in the long run. However, when arguing or disagreeing with someone you do care about, the words you use or the things you might say can make all the difference in the world. More importantly, all the difference in the future of the relationship.

Saying something deeply hurtful back to someone who has just hurt you verbally is how most people react. It's not necessarily planned, it's more like what happens in the heat of the battle; you hit me, I'm going to hit you back harder. It's easy to say things that will hurt someone when you truly know the person. You know where those wounds are, those deep scars that have not and perhaps will never heal. You know what is painfully embarrassing to them. You know things because you have a special relationship with this person. These things to anybody, would be defined as weak points; their "**Achilles Heels**." These things might be a secret to the world but not to you because of your relationship.

When I was growing up, there was a well-known saying,

"Sticks and stones might break my bones, but words will never hurt me." That's a lie, words can sometimes hurt more. There are too many hurtful examples of the damage words have caused. We see this played-out in the lives of young people being bullied on social media platforms, with sometimes devastating end results. Most broken bones over time heals, whereas some words said to certain people can have the power to create wounds that might never heal. Words are now and have always been extremely powerful.

When you have the privilege of being in a special relationship, be it with a family member or friend, you need to take special care in how you handle it. No matter how close the relationship, there are going to be times of disagreement, those are the times you need to activate this Achilles Heels concept. This is it; when you are arguing with someone you have deep feelings for, never-ever, ever-never, never-never, under any circumstances, no matter the reason, touch their "**Achilles Heels**." Find other ways to make your points, whether you lose or win the disagreement, the core of the relationship will probably remain solid.

The reason this approach works is because the opposite carries the promise of eroding and devaluing any and all relationships. When you attack someone's weak points, it reopens the hurt that originally caused the pain. Causing flashbacks to those situations carries the possibility of being problematic to the relationship going forward. Each time something like that occurs, it's like causing a crack in what was once solid, the more cracks, the less and less solid the relationship becomes. One day you wake-up and ask yourself, "What happened to us?" The use and misuse of words matter!

With the situation I questioned Mort on, he and his friend had words, his friend got upset with him, but the relationship remained intact. Mort knew where the boundaries were and was careful not to cross them with his friend. No matter the relationship or how close you are to someone, there will be times when there is friction. Often times that happens with the people we love the most because those are probably the ones we spend the most time with. The more you rub elbows with someone, the more opportunity for friction.

Everyone has experienced the joy of getting a new pair of shoes, that's typically not that big of a deal because we all wear and need them. With that being said, there have been times or maybe just that one time that most of us have experienced getting that special pair of shoes. That pair that stood out over all the rest for what could be a variety of reasons. It could have been the price or perhaps the style or maybe they were just the baddest pair of shoes you had ever seen, and you had to have them.

Now they're yours, you have your special shoes that you are only going to wear for special occasions and events. On one such occasion the shoes get scuffed. It hurts because they don't look or feel brand new now. However, they still mean a lot to you, so you make the necessary repairs and move on.

At some other point in time, they get damaged again; you get them repaired again. They still hold value for you but your feelings toward them are nothing like they were when you first put them on. If this scenario keeps repeating itself, at some point you will start asking yourself if the once cherished shoes are still worth fixing.

That is similar to what happens in relationships when you keep agitating a person's weakness with your words. Each time this happens, you are aware of the impact on the fellowship because you might not contact each other for a period of time. However, it might go unnoticed what is happening to the foundation of the relationship because this is not the first time something like this has happened. Truth is, you are slowly breaking down the relationship and over time, making that special someone see and feel differently about you. What might have been fun and comfortable is now changing.

When a relationship slowly breaks down, the severity as to what is happening might not get noticed until it is too late. When there is a big blowup that results in something unfixable, it stands out. Both parties know when and why the relationship is over. The big ones are a lot different than the little irritations that happen over time and slowly changes the relationship that has the ability to sneak up on you and catch you off guard. This is why being aware of Achilles Heels and properly applying the concept can be very vital to helping maintain relationships.

I remember being at a family picnic and a guest of one of my cousins coming up to me and declaring something he didn't understand. This was toward the end of the picnic, and he had been observing my interactions with family throughout the day. He said, "I don't understand why your family keeps hanging around you when you are so hard on them." I looked at him and laughed. This was my role reversal moment. He was me and I was Mort when I questioned Mort about how he talked to his friend.

This was simply Achilles Heels at work. I knew what I could and couldn't say to everyone I was interacting with. I knew when to pump the breaks to keep each encounter light and enjoyable. He probably heard me saying something to someone that sounded a little cruel. His wonderment was why this person not only wasn't upset but seemed to enjoy the moment. Part of it was my personality and the person knew me. The bigger part was that this person knew that I had never attacked their vulnerable points and felt comfortable, relaxed, and safe around me.

Not knowing about this concept but being someone that tries to avoid hurting people's feelings would gain you most of the benefits toward preserving relationships. While that is true, most of us have been in some heated verbal confrontations and there could be some in the future. The knowledge of Achilles Heels should now help to negotiate those difficult situations and safeguard the relationship long term.

What I just shared is what I learned from my study of Mort. I have since learned some other values and nuances of Achilles Heels. Like the dangers of unknowingly stumbling upon a person's weak point and having to deal with the consequences. This was another incident that happened when I was at Saglek Bay. As I look back, it seems like a lot of stuff happened during my one year there.

One night, at the NCO club, I was sitting at a table with some friends just enjoying the evening and the company. At some point, one of the guys asked another guy if he had any naked pictures of his wife. This startled everyone at the table, especially the guy the question was directed to. After an awkward silence, he said, "NO" and was accompanied with a stare that seemed to say I don't believe you're asking me some dumb shit like this. The fella that posed the question then reached into his back pocket and asked him if he wanted one.

Let me give this some context of time, there were no cell phones or social media platforms back then. Therefore, it didn't take long to understand that this was a joke. We all had an extended laugh and continued with our evening. The person he asked the question to seemed to enjoy it the most.

Several nights later, I'm back in the club sitting at a table socializing with a different set of friends. The mood is light, and we are having a good time. I remembered the joke from the other night and decided to pull it on someone I considered a friend. This guy would brag from time to time about some of his extra marital affairs, so he seemed perfect to be the object of the joke. He was a lifer, soft spoken, well liked, and I had never seen him upset; he also had a black belt in some discipline of martial arts. So here we go, I asked if he had any naked pictures of his wife. The table also got quiet, but it felt different than the silence of the other night.

His reply was, "What did you say?" That could have been and should have been my cue to explain that my question was tied to a joke I heard the other night. But oh no, I was dumb enough to repeat the question and let's just say that all hell broke loose at our table, and it was coming straight at me. Everything about him changed in an instant. I was sitting directly across from him. He started cussing, I had never heard him cuss before, then jumped up from the table and was trying to make his way around to my dumb ass. The other guys at the table restrained and talked him down. I explained the joke and apologized.

While he accepted my apology, our relationship took a hit. We were always cordial toward each other after that but we both knew that something had changed. My Achilles Heel take-away from what I call the "joke" is simple but important. Don't assume. If you have to wonder how a person is going to receive something you might say, leave it alone. Don't assume what the impact will be; you might be dangerously wrong.

Something else I learned about Achilles Heels has probably cost me a relationship with someone I care about. This is different than the "joke," I clearly knew her weak point, but this was more complicated. This had to do with a relationship between her and a man she had deep feelings for. This guy was her Achilles Heel. She knew it and so did I.

In the beginning, she was seeking my advice. We would talk for long periods about this guy. She understood that even if they were to reconnect, it would not be the same as before they separated. The trust in the relationship was gone; he had let her down too many times now. For several years he kept trying to get back with her. He would knock on her door at

3:00 a.m.; she would let him in to hear his new story. He was going to do better, he would go to rehab, he wasn't living with another woman, just to name a few promises. They were all consistently proven to be lies.

My friend is pretty, smart, had an incredibly good paying job, and was financially well off. At one point in time, most of the same could be said about this guy. Over time, our conversations became less frequent. We never did talk that often, but when we did, we would spend quality time catching up. Usually, at some point in the conversation, this guys' name would come up.

The change in our relationship was over this guy. I would always compliment her when she was strong and not open her door or take his calls. I would also remind her of who he had become whenever she would get weak for him. My position never changed toward the positive or the negative feedback to her. But something did change, and it went unnoticed to me. She stopped asking for my opinion, but I kept giving it when his name would come up, that proved to be a big mistake. While my message seldom changed, and she agreed with it, she was tired of hearing it.

Some people, at some point, grow weary of the truth. I believe that my voice had come to represent her Achilles Heel and her truth, and she stopped looking forward to hearing it.

She stopped returning my texts and calls. She might reach out to me one day, but for now the relationship has disappeared. Normally, I would have a defined take-way from an experience like this, this time I don't.

What I did learn is this, knowing someone's weak points and avoiding them is a lot different than helping someone deal with a weak point that is attached to a personal relationship. It's a lot more complicated and the input to that situation needs to be thoughtful, measured, and delicate. There are many situations and approaches to handling Achilles Heels. The one thing that most people will agree on is that our personal relationships are a big part of our lives and can make a huge difference in the quality of our lives.

The thing that I have grown to appreciate about this Achilles Heels concept is the lens it makes me look at life through. When I find myself in a conversation of disagreement with someone I care about, I adjust my tactics to not just get through the moment of discussion but rather to make sure that when the moment passes, and they always do, I have protected the relationship.

SEPARATION

You didn't have to spend a lot of time around Mort to feel that there was something different about him, something likable, something special. It's kind of like walking into some-one's home and getting a certain vibe. It could be that it feels warm and inviting, or perhaps you want to take your shoes off because you see the care the homeowner has taken with the spaces, or maybe you just like or dislike the house. Whatever you feel, it is tied to something.

After the initial first impression, the more time you spend in the home, it either confirms what you first felt, or it slowly changes your mind. Why? The answer is simple, time. The longer you are there, the more you see and dissect. Your opinion could be turned one way or another, relative to your first impression based on any number of things. It's not as clean as you first thought, or you really like their colors and accessory choices. What has happened is you are moving away from your feelings and more toward what you actually see, hear, and perhaps smell.

You see, I didn't need to take a deep dive into "who is Mort" to feel that he was special, which was my first impression, but I did need to spend time to find out why. I first came up with the "**BUTTONS**" and "**ACHILLES HEELS**" concepts but something kept telling me that there is more to this guy, much more that I had not yet identified. After many days and nights of bouncing between memories, I was finally able to put a label on what I was searching for.

I woke one morning, and it was clear as a loud bell to me, **"SEPARATION,"** that was the missing third piece. Mort had separated himself from all the people in his circle of influence and not just that but in his space period. The Buttons and Achilles Heels was part of it but only played a part, they were tools he used to help get separation in every phase of his life. The more I thought about it, the more I started to understand the importance and true value of separation.

In my preparation for writing on this subject, there was a period that I would ask people to respond to a question of mine. "What would be the one word to best describe the key to achieving your goals in life and why?" I preference the question by saying the word had to be from a secular perspective. You see, I know and talk to a lot of Christians and I'm sure that the majority of their answers would have been Jesus. Jesus is a great answer for many reasons, He represents the Bible and most of life's questions are answered through the inspired word of God. With Jesus not being an option, the word seemed to require a lot more thought.

The answers and rationale for them were somewhat predictable. For the most part, when you narrow the focus to one word, people tend to lean toward what they feel is the most important goal that would have the biggest impact on a successful or happy life. That makes perfect sense. Some of the answers were "Education," the rational being that with a good education would come a good job, a good job would bring good money, and money allows you to purchase the things and live the lifestyle you grew-up dreaming about.

Another popular answer was, "Love." The rationale being that without having reciprocal love in one's life (you loving people and them loving you), all of life's collectables and accomplishments wouldn't mean very much. There was a wide variety of words because people are individuals with varying goals. The bottom line is that there is no wrong answer.

The one troubling thing I found too often was the number of people that had no goals at all. Their rationale, "couldn't see past tomorrow, taking it one day at-a-time." I really think that in today's trials of trying to make it, there are many people that feel that way but won't admit it to others and sometimes to themselves. The more I thought about it, I think it's safe to say we all have experienced times like that in our lives.

Now I'm going to introduce you to my "one word" answer and the rationale to the question I posed: Separation. I believe that separation is not only a major key to achieving your goals but also the single most thing that impacts every facet of a person's life and lifestyle. Separation is happening all around us all the time whether we put a label on it or not, it's like the natural order or flow of life. Our world and society are set up to recognize and reward what this word stands for. Our station in life, for the most part, has everything to do with the reality and functionality of this word, separation.

Why do you think people who finish high school have more opportunities than those who drop out of school? Why do you think the people with a bachelor's degree make more money than the average person with only a high school diploma? Why master's degrees are more valued than bachelor's, and doctoral degrees more highly prized than master's?

You might tell yourself that the answer is intuitive, simple, or easy; the higher the education, the more it's valued, and you would be correct. Now, step back for a moment and look at the broader picture, society is telling us that there are different rewards for different levels of separation.

How do you think you wound up with the person you married? You might say that you got lucky, could be good luck or well, you know. Think about this, do you really think that you were their only option? The number of options doesn't matter, but what ultimately mattered was that during the courtship, you were able to achieve separation and became the final choice.

Separation is constantly on display in the world of sports, you see it played out at every level in all sporting activities. The more separation an athlete achieves in their sport, the more they are rewarded. In high school it's being a starter then making all-city and perhaps all-state honors. In college, it's getting your tuition free and the opportunity to play professionally. At the professional level everyone is good, so they strive to be great. There is a pay range for good with benefits and another for greatness.

Society lets everyone know who belongs in each category. The good gets paid, the great go to the "Hall of Fame" and have their uniform number retired and displayed in arenas. The harder you work, the more separation, the more separation, the more benefits.

Another one of the areas this plays out and has a major impact is on our jobs. I heard a story told once about a dad hearing what sounded like someone falling in one of the upstairs bedrooms. When he went up to investigate, he found that one of his sons had fallen out of the top bunk bed.

His question to the boy was simple, "What happened?"

His son's answer was also simple but also profound, he said, "I stayed too close to the getting in place." On most jobs, when you stay too close to where you first arrived, you are not taking advantage of possible opportunities within your place of employment.

Most people understand how this plays out, you get a job because you want and need to make money. Most people are not hired in at the top wage bracket but rather closer to the bottom. If you want more money, you have to find a way to move up the pay scale. You need to start working on ways to put this word into action, separation.

You need to start separating from everyone that is doing what you're doing, they're making the same money as you with the same job title. It does not matter the job nor the pay amount, you need separation to change your situation. You need the people around you to see and understand that there is something different, something special about you. You need to start standing out, you need to start separating!

In most workplaces, people want to move up to a more desirable place. A more desirable place will mean different things to different people, things like an easier job or perhaps a more challenging position that comes with more money and better perks. However, the problem gets to be either they don't know how, or they are willing to play what I call the lottery game. The lottery game is being positive, hoping that one day the right people will recognize their value and reward them. Good luck with that approach! I think that a better plan is to develop a strategy and make them see your value to a point where they can't ignore you.

I introduced this word and the concept behind it to a neighbor, Hobby. He was a young man in his early thirties with a wife and four young kids. One day he caught me in the yard and engaged me in a serious conversation. He was living with his in-laws, which didn't make him very happy. He was also stuck in what he called a dead-in job which made him depressed and miserable. I didn't try to address his living situation, but I did offer some advice as to what he was dealing with on his job. I started sharing the benefits of separation.

At that time, he and several other people were washing trucks at a local company. I began to tell him about the components of separation in the workplace. I explained the need to make his boss and other people that were making decisions in his work area see something different about him. I gave him several examples from my life. I then made it clear that the job itself and the number of people doing it does not change the basic principles and the benefits of getting separation. I suggested things like getting to work early, staying late, keeping his work area clean, and volunteering when opportunities presented themselves.

I also made it clear that separation does not mean you become a "yes man" with your nose stuck up your boss's behind. I left no doubt that people like that are not welcomed or wanted. We never talked about his two situations again. I probably didn't say "boss's behind" that day but I'm trying to use better language now; some days I'm more successful than others but I'm trying.

About two years later he bought a house in one of the neighboring suburbs and moved his family and mother-in-law to the new home. His father-in-law had died within that two-year span. He never told me that they were moving. One day I saw a moving truck and some activity at their house and went next door to see what was going on. He confirmed that he had bought a house but didn't say much else. There was a lot going on in the house, so I wished him well and went back home.

About a month later, I was outside in the yard when he pulled up and parked in front of his old house. He made the trip back partly because he had something he wanted to share with me. He began by thanking me for the encouragement and advice I had given him when we had that serious talk two years prior. He told me that he took my separation advice to heart and changed his whole attitude and approach to doing his job. He said almost immediately, things started to change for the better. He started moving up the ladder with better paying positions.

What he said next really made me feel good. He told me that my talk with him about separation was what made it possible for him to earn and save more money which made it possible to put the down payment on his new house. We hugged, and I let him know how proud I was of him and for him to keep marching in the same direction. I was also invited to any future BBQ parties.

Understanding how separation works is understanding both sides, there's the benefits side that comes from the working side. The working side is just that, it generally means that to get the benefits you have to work different than the people you are trying to separate from. The difference is what you have to figure out. It could be working harder, smarter, longer, more efficiently, or any number of other things. Finding ways to stand out really isn't that hard because the average person in the work force today is content with working just enough to get by. They are not looking to do anything extra. We all have examples of how separation has impacted our lives, we just never put a label on it.

While I don't know all the things that Mort did before we met, I know by his lifestyle, he made separation a priority. He probably called it something like "drive to do better," separation is my word for it.

As we travel down the road of life, we don't always know who is watching us or whose lives we might be impacting. Mort and I only knew each other for a few short months. He has no idea how he changed my life because we didn't stay in-touch with each other. When we said our goodbyes, as he boarded the plane, it was the last time we spoke or saw each other.

Truth is, we pass in and out of people's lives without the benefit of knowing the future. It's just another mystery of life. While maybe never having an official title as a mentor in someone's life, there still exist the real possibility of significantly impacting a life without ever knowing it.

In this chapter, I shared some things that have deep meanings for me. Principles I keep close that have helped me to be a better person. Buttons and Achilles Heels helped me with personal relationships. Separation was a constant reminder that I don't have to settle. If I don't like my situation, I should figure out a way to change it.

\

The winds of "**Separation**" are constantly blowing around us, it could be blowing in your favor or blowing against you. Sometimes it's a slight breeze and at other times it could be like a tornado. Understanding the Separation concept is understanding the difference between being proactive, trying to make an opportunity for yourself, and waiting around hoping and wishing for an opportunity that might never come your way.

CHAPTER 6

-FAMILY

Once you're in; you're never out!

There is history and stories to be told as to how each of our families got to where they are. However, I'm not interesting or unique enough to drive much curiosity about my family's genealogy. I'm not rich or famous enough. I've never been in a movie, and I don't drive a Bentley.

What I've chosen to talk about in this chapter, are things that relate to family issues. Things I've taken part in, and things I've witnessed, good things, bad things, great things, and tragic events.

At different times, we all take the occasional reflection on our lives and assess how we got to where we are. Often times, that assessment is weighted on how we feel at that moment. If things are going well, we tend to reflect on the positive. When we feel that things haven't gone our way, we focus on missed opportunities, bad breaks, and the darker side of life. What we reflect on at any given time could be the results of family interactions from as far back as our youth.

The family is a living structure. It has the ability to grow and shrink, to be inclusive, loving, and kind; or divisive, bitter, non-forgiving, and just hard to get along with. It can be strong and powerful while at the same time, be seen through the eyes of society as having perhaps a good or bad reputation, relative to how they choose to use that strength.

Each family member, whether they want to or not, has some liability and responsibility by their actions, which could either build up or tear down the family name, structure, and community standing. Each person's part in representing the family starts at an early age and never stops, you take it with you, everywhere you go and in everything that you do. The funny thing is, we hardly ever think about it, we just live our lives while this observance and evaluation follows us around.

Recognizing and understanding this type of scrutiny, and we all do from time to time, can be like a double-edged sword. One side can be good because it helps to keep us in line. The other can be bad because it can drive a person to act one way in public and another when they think they're out of sight from prying eyes. This can actually promote different personality traits. Perhaps a very buttoned down, presentable person in public might be found to have their house and home life in total disarray.

I believe that what gets poured into children helps to form the foundation of their mental psyche as they grow into adulthood. I also believe that when parents show love and build-up their kids to instill self-esteem and confidence, they tend to have a healthy mental image of themselves. Children growing up in abusive, unhealthy environments tend to reflect those scars as well. You hear professional people say that often times, when children are abused, they grow up to be child abusers.

I think that one of the more important roles of a parent is to be the counterbalance for their kids when it comes to self-esteem. The outside world has many numbers of tactics to beat a child down, both physical and mental. When that happens, parents need to step in to try and keep their children on solid, positive ground.

When our grandson was in middle school, our son and daughter-in-law were starting to worry about the growing attitude of their son. He was having a lot of success in sports within the private school system they had him in. They felt that all of the accolades and pats on the back was causing his head to swell. His self-esteem was off the charts, and it was starting to show. Being good parents and knowing that one day those pats on the back could possibly be replaced with words and actions of rejection, gave them concern about what they were seeing.

On one of their visits, we had a talk about that scenario and their concerns. I offered my take on the subject. I said, "Leave him alone, let him enjoy his time in the spotlight, nothing lasts forever." I reminded them about the world's potential for cruelty and its ability to beat a person down. I finally suggested that they get on board and build him up when warranted.

As he was approaching high school, he debated with his parents for several months about attending a large public high school. The school was known for its sporting achievements; it had many state titles. He wanted to be part of that and show off his skills. Finally, but reluctantly, they gave in and allowed him to attend the new school. He learned very quickly about the difference in skill levels between private and public schools. His last year at his private school, he broke the 100- and 200-meters track records at the school. For his first track season at the public school, they let him know they had heard about him. They then predicted that he might get to run a leg on one of the relays.

They were right. That first year, he ran a leg on a second

team relay; he wasn't used to that. He also played football for four years and didn't get to start until his senior year; he didn't like that either. I gave this example to show that when someone's self-esteem is healthy, they can better accept a few setbacks and not fall apart. In his senior year, the football team won the state title, and he made a key interception that helped propel them to victory.

That was one example that ended with positive results. It really could have turned out any number of ways; life comes with very few guarantees. It's for that reason, the unknown future, I believe it's always better to promote positivity because you never know when a child might need to draw from those reserves.

FAMILY MESS

Love, secrets, lies, betrayal, infidelity, abuse, gun violence, drugs, hatred, greed... These are not sub-plots to the next best-selling book or mega hit movie; this is some of the ingredients that makes up the family. Any part or combination of those mixtures are also known as "**Family Mess**."

Family Mess:

1. Mess within the family.
2. What an individual deems it to be.
3. You will recognize it when you either see it or are in it.

This is my simplified definition of that term. If you are of adult age and have no idea of what I'm talking about here, I have two things to say.

1. You and your family are very blessed.
2. Keep living, I promise you'll have some coming your way one day.

I am confident that no family can escape the reach of that two-word phrase forever. Here's why I say that. We all have to live in this world. In doing so, we all will face the sometime burden of witnessing some family mess. Every tragic story, reported on the local T.V. news station and in the newspaper, carries the possibility of creating "**Family Mess**." Every death, divorce, even weddings sometimes, could wind up in a bucket labeled "**Family Mess**." The mess is the stuff that carries negative disruptions within the family with the ability to tear it apart.

If you are still not sure if the "**Family Mess**" has invaded your family yet, here is a simple way to know. I call it the Thanksgiving/Christmas holiday mess test. Those two holidays, more than any others, separate families into three basic groups, which reflect the level of "**Family Mess**."

Here are the family groups.

1. Above average / exceptional.

2. Average / normal holiday stress.

3. Below average / dysfunctional.

Group one has everybody truly looking forward to the gathering and hoping that all loved ones are able to make it. I call this group exceptional because no one is anxious about the guest list, everybody gets along. It's going to be another family love fest. If someone cuts-up or drinks too much, no big deal. It will easily be handled. Minimal "**Family Mess**."

Group two is a toss-up. Anything could happen at any time. Most of the people coming have plans and hopes that everything will go well. They are also thinking that if a certain person shows up or this or that jumps off, it's going to be a problem, and they are not going to put up with it this year. I think that most families fall into that category at different times but for the most part, the holidays are O.K.; not great. I call this normal "**Family Mess**."

Group three is at a whole different level. A level at which metal detectors at the door would not be a bad idea. Half the family has a history of incidents with the other half and that history is bad when everyone is sober. When the drinking or smoking starts, and things get exaggerated, they have a designated person to call 911. I call these families dysfunctional. The password on most of their devices should be, family mess

911. Hardly anyone looks forward to these holidays. This is out of control "**Family Mess**."

One night at work, in those days I worked the afternoon or second shift, a co-worker approached me with a look on his face that wasn't normal for him. It seemed to be a look of concern or perhaps a pending decision that was weighing heavily on him.

We worked for a company that was tied to the auto industry. The fortunes of these types of industries are directly related to how well the economy is doing. If the country is experiencing a bustling, healthy economy, generally, people are buying new cars and companies like ours are doing well. Most of us are working overtime which drives fat paychecks. When the economy is down and struggling, our industry struggles; people are laid off. The auto industry is very cyclical like that.

At the time of the encounter with my co-worker, our company was laying people off in every plant and within every department. This included skilled trades, but the layoffs hadn't reached the tool rooms yet, which is where we worked. My first thoughts at interpreting his facial expression was that he was worried about being laid off, that seemed to be the topic of conversation throughout the plants. However, I misread the look, I was wrong.

I asked if he was O.K. He began to open up and our conversation went in a direction that was surprising and totally unexpected. His obvious distress was the result of him having an ongoing affair with his brother's wife, not ex-wife, but current. He was also married at the time. At some point, I asked about the possible impact or effect this might have on his family if the affair was ever exposed. His response was also unexpected.

When I posed that question, his demeanor shifted from concern to anger. This is what he said, "Families are like assholes, everybody has one, and they are not all good." He went on to say, "Within every family, there are always a few assholes, and I guess I'm one of them." Clearly, "**Family Mess**" issues here.

We talked for about an hour that night and I came away with a question that I asked myself from time to time, and still today, I seem to revisit it. It wasn't a question about his affair, people cheat all the time, even though that was close to home. The question was, "Why me?" Why would he share something that personal with me? We weren't friends, we only talked occasionally; we were just co-workers.

One of the reasons I would occasionally probe and revisit that question, "Why me?" is tied to my opinion about some things that go on within most churches. Church members would sooner share personal things with co-workers or a total stranger before they would with most fellow church members.

This is my take on why I believe that to be true. At first glance, that conclusion seems to cut against the grain of what should be the very essence and culture of what the church is supposed to represent. However, the majority of the members don't believe that the majority of the members would safeguard those personal conversations and issues. To that end, I believe my co-worker opening up to me that night was because we didn't run in the same circles, except at work. He knew that I didn't know his family or real friends; he felt safe with me. I didn't have the ability to hurt him where it mattered the most.

Sometimes, I see church and church people like I do prison and prisoners. With prisoners, after some time served, there should be signs and evidence of some rehabilitation. After time spent in the church, there should be signs and some evidence of Christian growth. Sometimes there is and sometimes there isn't. When there isn't, it carries the possibility of creating "Church Family Mess." I probably should change the subject now; so, I will.

Most people walking down the aisle getting married are probably not thinking about divorce, but it happens. Bad things that happen within families all have a common denominator, living life. Life happens. We want what we can't have, we buy what we can't afford, we go where we shouldn't be, we say and do hurtful things, and on and on and on until life gets to be some form of "**Family Mess**." These are things we have some control over. Then there are the various addictions that are no brainer, "**Family Mess**" stuff.

We can find ourselves in the middle of some mess through no fault of our own. As an individual, trying to resolve family problems can sometimes be as hard as trying to push a rope. That's because the only thing we can really control is ourselves. If someone would have told me that I would one day be estranged from my daughter, I would have found that laughable, but it happened. I'm grateful that we fought our way back to each other. Now, I can't imagine my life without her in it.

"**Family Mess**" is like your shadow. You don't always see it, but if you put yourself in the right or wrong situation, it can and probably will show up.

PERSONAL

I'm the product of a loving, close, six-member family (my parents, two sisters and a brother). My sister Gwen is the oldest, followed by me, my sister Arbor, and youngest brother Anthony/Tony/Dink. As kids we interacted like most siblings do, the occasional roughhouse but nothing crazy.

As you see, Anthony had a few nicknames and so did I. My grandfather called me, "Tojo, Bombshell, Council Rock, Squirrel." Most people called me Tojo. My father called me Toe. When I started attending school, the teacher called me Fred. Sometimes, when she called out, "Fred," I wouldn't respond because I didn't remember that was me.

Growing up in my youth/pre-teen years, was very special. It was summer days spent with non-stop outside activities at Bailey Park, which was at the end of our street, mixed in with quality family fellowship. That was mostly eating and fishing, as I recall, eating across the street at my grandparent's house. My grandmother, Little Ma liked to cook and my grandfather, Big Daddy, or Hick Daddy, always had a watermelon at the ready. He tried to teach all of us kids how to thump the melons to tell how ripe they were. That was a lesson I never learned because it would hurt my fingers, so I gave up trying. When I go to buy a watermelon now, I regret my failure at that task because it's 50-50 now at me picking a good one.

Then there was my two uncles, they lived on either side of my grandparent's house. I liked watching and learning how to build things from my Uncle James. He was very good at making stuff with his hands and seemed to like having me around when he was working on something. He was also an avid hunter. I never wanted to tag along for that, and I didn't/

never liked fooling with guns.

My other uncle was Joe, Uncle Joe. I spent more time with him than I did with my father and Uncle James combined, that was mostly because he was the one that took me fishing all summer. We would go one-on-one sometimes and then there were the "Picnic Fishing" events that would happen on some weekends. Those were my versions of "Disneyland," I loved them. Anybody that wanted to come was welcomed, and we would generally wind up with a party between six and eight.

Most of those weekend trips would be to Lake Erie. The drive was over an hour long with a stop at a bait/convenience store, that's when the fun started for me. That stop meant that we were in the city of Ashtabula where we would be fishing, and it was time to load up on the sweets, big fun!

Uncle Joe also taught me how to box. He was a big guy and boxed as a "Heavy Weight." His boxing was mostly in the "Golden Gloves" tournaments. One of my fondest memories was going to a match at the Struthers Fieldhouse with him and my Aunt Maggie, his wife, my mother's sister. When we got out of the car, I asked if I could carry his gym bag, and he tossed it to me. I felt like we were a team; big deal for me! I learned a good lesson that night. He won the fight by knocking out his opponent in the second round. On the way back to the car, I asked him about the fight. What he said had a lasting impact on me.

He said he knew he was a better fighter, but in the first round the guy hit him with a punch that he didn't see coming and it hurt him. That made him fight harder in the second round to try and take him out. He then turned to me and said, "Just because you're the better fighter, does not mean that you are going to win." He made it clear, that when you are in a fight, there are no guarantees. That was the lesson for me.

We've all heard people say, mostly in jest, "I'm not a fighter, I'm a lover." Back then I wasn't a "fighter" or "lover," I was more of a talker. My uncle instilled a certain self-confidence in me that I could handle myself if it came to a fight, but I would rather talk first. I always felt that I liked my odds, but I never forgot that better does not mean victory.

Our mother was the heartbeat and stabilizing force of our family. She was loving but tough at the same time. I think growing up, I experienced more of her tough side than my brother and sisters put together. There is one that stands out to this day, she said it was because I had a hard head. I was saying to myself, I will hate you for the rest of my life if you make me do this!

Us kids had to be in the house when or before the streetlights came on. I missed that curfew two days in a row. The first day, I got a tongue-lashing that ended with a, "It better not happen again!" When I came home late that second day, I really didn't know what I had waiting on me, I just knew it wouldn't be good. To my surprise, nothing happened. I walked right pass her, and she never said a word. I didn't want to press my luck, so I went straight to bed.

When I got up the next morning, I couldn't find my clothes, there was only one of my sister's dresses on the chair in the corner. When I got tired of looking, I hollered downstairs to my mother, "I can't find my clothes."

She came upstairs and changed my life for a day. She pointed to that chair in the corner and explained that the dress was what I was going to be wearing all day. She did give me an option though, I started to smile because I thought it was going to be a whipping with a switch, I was used to that. I was wrong. She said, "Put on the dress or you can't live here anymore."

I put the dress on and I'm thinking that I would just sit around the house all day, wrong again. When I came downstairs she told me to keep walking. Then she said, "Every time I look out one of these windows I better see you. You better not be hiding." Like I said, she was tough! I was never late getting home for the rest of the summer. If you did something wrong, she never said, "Wait 'til your father comes home." She took care of your behind, right then and there!

Our father probably thought that he was raising little saints. He never got to whip us. Our mother had all the fun, except for this one time. He got to do me, and it turned out that he didn't know how. It's dinner time and we were out of Kool-Aid. He wanted me to go to the corner store and get some. It was winter, and cold outside. I didn't say "No," but I went and hid in the closet in their bedroom. After some time had gone by, he noticed that I hadn't taken the money off the table. He knew that I had not left the house, and he was pissed. The search for me was on.

The house didn't have many hiding places. It didn't take them long to find me. He took off his belt and proceeded to beat me with it. Somehow, the belt got twisted and he hit me with the buckle. It put a hole in the top of my foot, and it started to bleed, I didn't have any shoes on. He felt bad but was trying to convince me that the hole in my foot was my fault, that was the first and last time I felt his belt.

Growing up, my father and I didn't spend much time together. I wouldn't say that we were distant, it was more like we weren't close. I always loved my father, but I didn't always like him. At some point, I felt that he cared more about his image with people outside the house than he did with the people inside his household. He and my mother divorced when I was in high school which catapulted him to the top of my "shit list." Somewhere during the time periods of him moving to New Jersey and me starting a family, we became very close. Over time, he became my closest confident and proved to be a great guy with a big heart. I grew proud to call him, "My father."

The tough image of my mother has always been a permanent description of her to me. So, imagine my surprise when I'm in my mid-forties and I find out that she had a nervous breakdown when we were kids. I remembered one summer I was sent to live with my father's brother's family on another side of town for a period of time (Uncle Bill, Aunt Marie, and my cousins Brenda and Keith). My mother had went to New Jersey to get herself together that summer. Thinking back on those forty plus years, didn't change my image of her. In fact, knowing some of the things she had to deal with, let me know that she was even stronger than I had imagined.

We all knew that her love for us was even wider and deeper than her toughness. She was our rock. We always knew that we could count on her, no matter what. She was my tower-of-strength example, and we all loved her dearly.

After I retired, I had an occasion to do lunch with a friend I knew from work who was also retired. It was a good time eating, laughing, and catching up, we talked about some work stuff but most of the conversation was geared toward our families. We had a hard time acknowledging how old we were as we pondered and discussed where all the time went. We only knew each other from work, so we weren't familiar with each other's backgrounds growing up. One of the things I shared was the uniqueness of my living situation as a child, how our house, my grandparent's house, aunt's, and uncle's houses were all next to each other. I painted a picture that would be worthy of a child-friendly, Walt Disney film; how close we were as a family and that it seemed like a non-stop love fest (there were seven cousins also in that mix).

Lunch is over and I'm driving home when the memories from the past collided with reality. That idyllic world growing up, that I Disneyland through, turned out to be something much different for my adult chaperones that I loved.

They were all divorced, my parents, aunts, uncles, and probably my grandparents if my grandfather hadn't died. I was surrounded with "**Family Mess**," when I was a child, and never knew it. I'm glad it didn't surface until I was older because my childhood memories are still something I cherish.

MY TRACK MEET MYSTERY

Something happened to me in high school that also went unnoticed for a long time, somewhat of a mystery. It's late May 1965, my senior year. Track season is wrapping up and it's

Friday. This is the day of the city-wide finals to be contested under the lights at the Rayen Stadium, in Youngstown, Ohio. The qualifiers/prelims were held the previous Wednesday.

During the lunch period at school, one of the coaches told me that I had the fastest qualifying time Wednesday in the high hurdles. This was news to me because I never followed the season's meet times in the newspaper. I was pumped at that news because it made me feel like I had a legitimate shot at winning later that night. I say it that way because everybody knew that the best time in the qualifiers does not always represent the fastest runner.

I had an up and down season that year with inconsistent times in the high and low hurdles from meet to meet. However, I did break our school's low hurdle record that year and broke the high's in my junior year. While I was proud of my accomplishments, my records didn't mirror those that stood for the city or state. There was one other thing that I was proud of, I always gave my all at each meet, win or lose. That effort is somewhat at the heart of this mystery.

It's Friday night at the stadium, the stands are full. Track has always been a big deal within the inner-city schools with fierce competition in each event. The high hurdles are always ran first, and the meet is about to start. My warm-up routine was always the same, I would high step the first four or five hurdles, go back and actually run four or five, depending on how I felt. Something changed within me that night when I finished the warm-up run and was walking back to the starting line. I glanced up at the crowded stands and had what felt like an out-of-body experience. It was like I was as empty as the stands were full.

My race is about to start. The starter announced, "Runners, stand up in your lanes." At that point, I remember slapping my right thigh and saying to myself, "Come-on Fred, this is the finals, let's go," but I felt nothing. With all the track I had run over the past four years, I had never experienced anything like that feeling before. It wasn't a nervous feeling; I had felt that plenty of times before and could easily recognize it. This was more like a nothing feeling; like a why am I here?

The start gun finally goes off; I came in third place. I ran the low hurdles later that night and also ran a bad race. The losing during those finals didn't haunt me for years, but that unexplainable feeling that came over me did. You see, I had lost races before, but that feeling was new for me, and I didn't know why. That experience was a mystery that took me over six years to solve.

Now I'm out of the military, married, and living with my in-laws. We lived with them for a year to save for a down payment on our first home. There was a family celebration of someone's birthday and some family members are over. I was in the living room showing my wife's uncle and grandfather the new and latest audio equipment that I had brought home from the military. At some point during that demonstration, the conversation shifted to football and led to my track mystery being solved.

Her uncle and grandfather were both named Lingar Humphrey, junior and senior. We called senior, "Pops." Junior was an outstanding football player in the city and earned a college scholarship. During that conversation, Junior said that his father never missed a game of his, home or away. He went on to say that he was never in the stands but rather on the field, up and down the side-lines for every play. When he said that, a light turned on for me that heavily influenced how I raised and interacted with my kids. Lingar emphasized how much it meant to him to have his dad at the games. He mentioned things like when he would get tired, look over at his father, and get re-energized.

My entire four years of playing high school sports (football and track) neither of my parents ever saw me in a uniform. They were never at a football game, never at a track meet. My father gets a pass for my junior and senior years because he and my mother were divorced, and he had moved out of state by then. I do remember one uncle coming to one football game.

It would be fair to think that this should never have been a mystery. It would be fair to assume that the reason I felt like that should have been obvious, your parents are missing. Yes, my parents were not there that night, but neither were the parents of the friends that I hung with. You see, we never looked for our parents. We played because we wanted to play. For those reasons, that last track meet should not have raised a red flag like that for me. Their absence should not have caused the anxiety that I experienced, but it did. I had nothing to prove to anyone in those stands, they saw me run on Wednesday and I ran well.

I wrote about a homework assignment at my current church in the chapter, "How a mentor changed my life." Part of that assignment was to name three people that had the greatest influence on my life. I wrote that one of the persons I chose would probably come as a complete surprise to my family if they knew about this exercise. That's because Lingar and I were not close, the only time we would interact would be at family events which didn't happen very often.

Because he and I were not close, I never shared the impact that football conversation had on me, but it was profound. When my kids were involved in sports, or anything else, so was I. I don't remember ever missing an event. Our son played pee wee and high school football, never missed a game. He ran track in high school, never missed a meet. Kevin was also into martial arts. I missed a tournament in Cleveland once because he wanted to ride with the coach and some of the other kids. Our daughter was a majorette in high school, never missed a halftime baton twirl. Lingar deserved to be on my list of three.

"People get used to what you get them used to." This is one of life's truisms that I have come to embrace. My parents had gotten me used to them not being at my events, that was my normal. I don't think that I ever thought that much about, that is, until that last meet. That feeling, when I looked in the stands, felt abnormal. That night, I wanted someone up there for me.

After that day spent with the Lingars, I knew what I wanted and felt like I needed to do for my kids, be there, show up. I wanted them to know that there would always be someone either in the audience or in the stands for them. This was going to be one of the ways that I felt family interaction should look and feel like. Sometimes, some of the things that happen to you, happen for you!

I would like to think that my approach had some effect on our son and daughter because they are very active in supporting their kids. It makes me extremely proud to know and see that.

I think that if I ever had to defend why I like to engage with people in conversation, especially strangers, this Lingar situation would be one that I would point to. I'm always amazed at some of the things people are doing and have done with their lives, especially some of their hobbies. I like finding out how people pay the bills, but their hobbies tell you what they are passionate about. Some conversations can be very eye opening like the one I had with the Lingars.

PENDING DIVORCE; *Mine*

Life happens, and decisions are made; all the decisions we make are based on some matter of context. What I mean is simply this, each decision we make in real time is based on something, that something is part of our decision-making process. Even impulsive, seemingly pulling it out of thin air decisions are based on something. Another way of saying it is this, "None of the decisions we make are based on nothing, they are all based on something."

We wake in the morning shower, brush our teeth, and put on clothes. This gets to be part of our daily routine, part of our daily thought routine. Those are some things that we do without giving much thought to, except perhaps the putting on the clothes part. Even the dailies are driven by context or reasons, we shower and brush our teeth because we like to feel clean and fresh. We put on clothes because most of us don't live in nudist colonies for one thing; another is because most of us look better covered up.

If you are now starting to wonder and question why I've drifted into this topic on context, in the middle of a chapter on Family, it would make you normal. It looks a bit out of place, I'll explain the placement.

In the chapter, "**Growing up in the USAF**," I declared that I was going home to get a divorce. What I shared in that chapter, seemed like I was willing to end my marriage of less than two years over two missed late-night calls, back home to my wife that now had a six-month old baby boy. From the outside looking in it might seem impulsive and perhaps irrational. However, to me, my decision had merit because of the context attached to it. While to most people, it would seem like a giant leap, going from two missed calls to divorce, but to me, it was more like stepping over a small crack in the sidewalk. I was just connecting the dots.

Everything we experience goes into the archives of our minds; they are always there because something actually happened. That experience didn't have to happen to us, but it was absorbed in our minds. Some of those are always easy to recall and some seem to fade away. The ones that have been suppressed may have been because of the time elapsed since the incident, it could also be because it is something you really want to forget. However, even those faded or forgotten memories of the past can sometimes be triggered to surface by something that might happen in real time, the present regurgitating something from the past. All of our memories/experiences, adds to our context/reasons, for our decision making.

There were three things that had context in my past that added greatly to my decision to want to divorce my wife, cut my losses, and move on.

Context #1

I never had an official girlfriend in high school, that was mostly because of what I experienced in high school. I had plenty of friends like everyone else, that were girls, but none I liked or trusted enough to get high school serious about. That's right, I had trust issues in high school and for what I deemed to be good reasons.

While I didn't have a girlfriend, from time to time I was spending quality time with other guy's girlfriends. These were never relationships that I pursued but at the same time, I hardly said, "No," to an advancement coming my way. I would sometimes be with girls on the weekend and see them walking the halls in school on Monday with their boyfriends, acting like they were the love of their lives. I was never a kiss-and-tell person. However, when I would see the weekend girl versus school day girl scenario play out, I would sometimes smile to myself and think about how devious, conniving, and sneaky girls can be.

While I seemed to be on the better side of those situations, it didn't take a lot of imagination to see things reversed; with me possibly on the other side of that fake love.

Context #2

It was the summer after I graduated, my future wife would be starting her senior year of high school in the fall. We were introduced by a mutual friend at a downtown skating arena. Her name was Sandra, and I called her "San." That friend would later become my "Best man" at our wedding. We had been dating about three weeks. It's Saturday and I'm coming over to pick her up. We were going to a party at one of her girl-friend's houses that lived on her side of town.

When I got to her apartment it was dusk, but the streetlights are on. As I pulled up to the curb, I noticed four or five guys talking as they surrounded a car. That car was under the street-light across from where I was parked. I almost spoke but this was a side of town where I didn't know many people, so I just went up and rang San's doorbell.

As we were leaving, heading to the party, I heard her mother say, "Be careful, you know that (then she called out a name) is home." San didn't reply, and I pretended like I didn't hear anything. When we get outside, the car across the street and all the fellas were gone.

We thought that it was too early to go to the party and agreed to just ride around for a while. We're still on her side of town when I turned on to a street and suddenly found myself surrounded. A car came up from behind, sped up, turned in front of us, and blocked my way forward. I slammed on the breaks. It's the same car that was under the streetlight.

My engine is still running. Everybody gets out of that car and are walking in the street toward us. I look over at San and asked," Do you know these guys?"

She said," That's my ex-boyfriend's car. He's in the Air Force."

He walks up to my window, pulls his pants up an inch or two, and said, "Let me introduce myself." At that point, I put the car in reverse and got the hell up out of there. They didn't try to follow us.

We were on the North Side of town where she lived. I drove to my house on the East/Sharon Line Side of town. I pulled up the driveway and told San to stay in the car. I went inside, got a summer jacket, my mother's gun/pistol, got back in the car, and backed down the driveway. At the first stop sign, I rolled my window down, pointed the gun to the sky, and pulled off a round; I wanted to make sure that it worked. That shot startled San and now she is more scared than she was earlier. She asked where we were going. I said, "To the party." She didn't want to go, but I insisted. At that point, I didn't know how the evening was going to end, but I knew that I was done running.

I stayed seated most of the night with my eyes locked on the front door. The carpool with all of the so-call tough guys never showed. Sometimes, when I think back on that night, I get a knot in my stomach and thank God for what didn't happen. I say that because, that night I was embarrassed and mad as hell, mostly mad. If they had walked in that door, lives would have changed, mine for sure.

That happened on Saturday, that Monday, after work, I asked a friend if he would help me get some stuff straightened out. He said, "Yes," and we headed for the North Side. I spotted one of the guys with some of his friends gathered in front of a store; I was told that it was one of the hang-out spots. I still had the gun, but it was left in the car. My friend and I get out, I walked up to the guy I recognized from Saturday, threatened him, and asked where the Air Force guy was. He explained that he didn't want any trouble, that he was just with his friend, and he had gone back to his Air Force base. I told him to let his friend know that I looked forward to seeing him the next time he comes to town. While we never saw each other again, we did have an encounter via the U. S. postal service.

The next time I saw San, she said something that is actually my second point of context. Her words were meant to be comforting and reassuring but they had the opposite effect on me. She said that she sometimes has two boyfriends at the same time, but that I would be her only one going forward. I didn't know her well enough or long enough to even respond. I thought to myself, "Time will tell," but her statement, to me, had a bit of a smell to it. I've always believed that if you do something once, you are capable of doing it again!

Context #3

Also, in the chapter "Growing up in the USAF," I wrote about a letter I received during my basic training. The letter talked about what San was doing back home in Youngstown. The last statement in the letter was, "I'm not saying she's cheating on you but what do you think?" I figured out that it was from her Air Force ex. At that time, I considered the source, laughed, and dismissed the letter. I never talked about it again. When I went home for the first time, I never mentioned it to San.

Ignoring that letter was something I chose to do. However, our minds are not like an Etch-a-Sketch toy where you can totally erase something and move on. Because I read it, it was now registered somewhere inside my head. That meant that there was always the possibility that it could surface, no matter how deep I tried to bury it. Those two calls home unearthed that letter and became part of my decision to divorce along with context #1 and #2.

I was faced with a very daunting decision as I was processing out of the military, returning to civilian life, and my family. The decision did not carry with it a lot of options, only two; divorce or stay married. Weighing the context of the past against the truth of the present to determine my future life's path was beginning to overwhelm me. The decision, with all of its future implications was fast approaching overload for my small to medium hat size head to handle. The truth of the present that I'm speaking about was this; I now had a six-month old baby boy and I'm questioning my love for my wife.

When I got discharged from the Air Force, and found myself back home in Youngstown, my upper most thought was not focused on loving my wife and seeing my baby boy; it was on divorce. I was consumed with it. Everything seemed off, everything was awkward and strained. It was not a fun time for either of us. This went on for nearly three weeks; no touching, no conversation, except when others were around, and a constant questioning of my true feelings for her. Finally, the tension got to be too much, some decisions needed to be made. I told her that we needed to have a serious talk about our family's future; she agreed.

While I wasn't sure of my feelings for my wife, there was one thing that I was rock solid sure of; no man was going to raise my son but me! This was going to be a conversation with life-changing possibilities. I don't know how long we talked but it felt like forever. My words were harsh and to the point. Her words were tearful, loving, apologetic, and hopeful. By the time our session was over, we had both shed a few tears. We decided that there was still enough love remaining to give our family another chance; divorce was off the table. While I was speculating as to what she might have done, the regret for my one-night infidelity was continuing to mount and that also played a role in my decision.

Being many years now, on the other side of that conversation and decision, I'm convinced that it was the right and best decision of my entire life! Sometimes when I look at my beautiful daughter and her son, I'm reminded of the possible implications all of our decisions could have on our futures. She was born five years after we decided to stick it out. I thank God that He gave us the wisdom to get that one right.

A LONG GOODBYE

My first long goodbye was devastating for me and the family. The goodbye that I'm sharing is the one between me and my first wife. She died July 10th, 1990. We were married for twenty-two years, and she was forty-two years old. She was first diagnosed in 1986 with breast cancer. She underwent chemotherapy; it went into remission then came back in 1989. Her condition took a turn for the worse in early 1990. That's when I started trying to imagine our lives without her in it. This was difficult because she was a wonderful person, a wonderful wife, and the best mother any child could ask for. She had given us a great life.

I'm not gifted enough, articulate enough, and my personal lexicon isn't deep enough to paint an accurate word picture as to what happened to me on July 10, 1990. I just know that I changed. I also know that I'm not the same person today that I was before her death.

Her first diagnosis happened when she was in the operating room for a breast lumpectomy. The test results came back malignant. After considering the options, we made the decision to do a mastectomy; that breast was removed. After that surgery, the doctor reported that they felt that they had removed all of the cancer cells. I remember feeling relieved. I was ready to turn the page and get on with our lives.

My wife, San, worked for an insurance company handling various insurance claims. While I was happily moving on, she was starting to get concerned about the lack of follow-up instructions. She knew that in most breast cancer surgeries, there was either follow-up with chemotherapy, radiation, or both. Three weeks had gone by, she voiced her concerns to me and the next day we were making phone calls.

We discovered that the ball had been dropped. The surgeon thought that her medical doctor was going to follow-up with further treatment options, and he thought the surgeon was going to make recommendations; not good. Because of the time lapse, her medical doctor recommended that we go to Cleveland Clinic to consult with their cancer experts for future treatment options. Cleveland Clinic is world renowned for most of their services, but for us it was a confusing disaster. We had appointments with three different doctors and each one gave us slightly different directions. We came back home and settled on chemotherapy treatments.

That treatment pursuit left a bad taste in our mouths and led to me making her a promise. I told her that if the cancer should come back, we were not going to deal with anybody in this area. I did some homework and discovered that one of the leading cancer centers in the country was in Buffalo, New

York; Roswell Park.

When her cancer came back, I bought a van so that she could be comfortable, and we made plans and appointments to go to Buffalo. From that point on, most of her reports were up and down; from stable to moving in the wrong direction. Even the way she found out that it had returned was cruel and poorly handled. I was at work, a few minutes away from leaving my office to go to a staff meeting within my Superintendent's area. All of us supervisors were giving presentations. San calls. When I answered the phone, I could tell that she had been crying. I knew that she had a doctor's appointment to get the results of her last scheduled cancer check-up. I asked what was wrong. She only said, "I need you to come home." I went to my meeting, explained that I needed to be first up and that I would be taking the rest of the day off.

When I got home, she told me what had happened, and my first reaction went from concern to anger. She said that the doctor came in the room with her report, told her that the cancer had come back, and that it was bad! He didn't ask if anyone was with her to drive her home, just hit her in the face with that report. He showed her no mercy, no compassion. He next stated that they would schedule an appointment for options to consider. She said that she left the hospital, sat in the parking lot, and cried for most of twenty minutes. Luckily, we lived only five minutes away. I wanted to get in my car and go back to the hospital and raise some serious hell, but I knew that I was needed at home. She never went back to that hospital for cancer treatments.

We made three trips to Buffalo; the last one was heartbreaking for both of us. She was always upbeat, that was one of the things that I loved about her and this visit was no different. When they called her name, she didn't want me to go back with her. At that time, I didn't want to push her, so I said, "O.K." She went in smiling, came out smiling twenty-five minutes later. By the time she came out, I had changed my mind, I wanted to talk to the doctor. She didn't try to stop me. The doctor and I talked for a few minutes then we headed back to Ohio. What he told me made for a long, quiet ride home.

He told me that San was terrific and a woman of deep faith. He further stated that a positive attitude can make a big difference when people are dealing with serious health issues. He said that he didn't want to mess with that, and he got the impression she didn't want him to. I thanked him for respecting her faith and treating her kindly, but I wanted his opinion on her prognosis. You see, she had been there for over five hours taking tests. He said that they weren't getting the results for which they were hoping. His next statement was a game changer. He said, based on what the tests revealed, unless there was a dramatic change or a miracle, he would give her about six months; could be more, could be less.

There wasn't much conversation on the ride home. She knew something was off with me. When we got home and were taking our coats off in the hallway, she said, "He told you something, didn't he?"

My response was, "Only God knows when we are leaving here."

She pressed me again, "I want to know what he said!" I told her that he said, if things don't turn around for her, she wouldn't make it past ten years. She broke down like I had never seen her before. She cried, I cried, and we held each other in that hallway like we were saying goodbye; that's what it felt like for me. I often thought to myself, if she reacted like that with a ten-year answer, what would she have done if I had told her the truth. She lived another three months.

When the end was near, she was back in the hospital in Youngstown. My brother came in from Kanas City to help support me and the family. The night before she passed, they had her on heavy drugs to keep her comfortable. She had a tube in her nose that she kept trying to pull at. They were talking about putting shackles on her wrists to prevent her from pulling the tube out. I said, "NO!" My brother and I stood by her bedside all night. We were talking to each other, talking to her, praying, going down memory lane, and protecting that tube. It was a long night, and I will be forever grateful for how my brother stood with me that night; he was a difference maker. Kevin, our son, was still at his college campus. I didn't want him to see his mother like that. Nicole, our daughter, was in town, I couldn't keep her away.

That morning I went home to get a shower and some needed sleep, anticipating another long, goodbye night. I returned to the hospital about mid-afternoon. When I got off the elevator, I saw a crowd gathered in the hallway outside of her room. A strange feeling came over me. Each step seemed labored. It felt like my heart was trying to skip beats, I could hardly breathe. My Uncle James broke away from the crowd, met me halfway down the hall, and said, "She's gone."

My family didn't let the hospital staff move her. They knew that I would want some final goodbye time with her, and I was thankful. I went in the room, the door closed behind me. She looked like she was sleeping. I held her hand and we started talking, actually just me, but I could almost hear and feel her responses. I began thanking her for everything I could think of. For her being the Christian woman that she was, for loving me, for being the loving mother of our kids, and so much more. I called myself reminding her of how much she was loved and would be missed.

I remember the last things I said to her. I thanked her for showing me how to die with dignity and trusting God to the end. Part of my last goodbye was a promise to protect the kids and that we would do our best to make her proud of us. With that, I kissed her gently and told her that I would see her in heaven. My heart was broken; I was crushed but there were things that needed to be done.

After thanking everyone that was there and finishing the necessary paperwork at the hospital, I finally left and headed to my grandmother's house. She was not at the hospital, and I wanted to tell her face to face. She loved San, too.

On my way, I stopped at a red light and glanced over at the car that was beside me in the other lane. It appeared to be a mother and daughter. They were laughing and talking while looking back and forth at each other. Seeing that made me feel like, not only were we in separate cars, it seemed like we were in separate worlds. My world was falling apart, but for them, it was just another day.

On my way home from my grandmother's, I thought about the car that was next to me and wondered why it was still on my mind. I questioned how and why I could have room for any thoughts other than what I had just experienced. I pulled into the garage and just sat there. It was like I couldn't move until I solved the mystery of the scene in that car. It was like the Lord had a message for me and I was desperate to hear it.

When I opened the car door and went in the house, the message seemed clear and so did my direction. It was this, at this time; there are two worlds for me, my world of pain and grief and the one that I would have to move forward in. It was telling me that the pain was real but don't stay there; I have too many people counting on me. I needed to find/fight/claw my way back to that other car, that other world, and not take forever to get there.

FAMILY REUNION

Now that I'm in my golden years, my perspective on family has become clearer than it ever has at any other time in my life. I've always had a strong appreciation/love for family and felt that it was special and needed to be defended and protected. However, now when I look back at my life and times, I tend to view family ties and memories as a life-long scavenger/treasure hunt.

I have come to believe and understand that God has placed people in our lives for a reason; that includes family, friends, and others. The real key is trying to solve the mystery as to why He placed them there. More specifically, what cause and effect did He purpose to impact our lives; some seem to be more obvious than others.

When your mind starts down that path, you can't help but wonder, did I interact with the people that crossed my path the way that God intended? I say that because I know that God gives each of us the free will to make our own decisions. Part of that wonderment stirs questions like, how many times did I turn left when He desired me to turn right? How many relationships did I keep at a distance when He intended me to cultivate and nurture? This is something none of us will ever know for sure.

I guess one approach would be to treat everyone like you would want to be treated. If that was the way we always treated people, then we would have no nagging after-thoughts about who is and isn't in our lives. Truth is, we don't always treat everyone like that. Sometimes, we have treated some family and others with some level of disdain, disgust, disappointment, and down-right hatred. The sad part of that scenario is that we have justified it in our minds; so and so did this and that and deserves exactly what they got from me. These types of feelings tend to separate people and break down relationships.

Maybe the people in or out of our lives are the ones that God intended for us to either draw close to or stay away from. The point I'm trying to make is that we shouldn't beat ourselves up over our current situation relative to who we are close to or distant from. There will always be people in those positions in our lives. Although going forward, I would suggest that we test the people we interact with and that crosses our paths. This is the test, take people at face value until they prove to be otherwise. That means when you meet someone, don't automatically put the label on them that some others have told you that they should have. There could be many reasons people might say things about a person. Some might be personal, some hear-say, and some could be the truth about the person, at least their truth.

Start with a blank slate, the truth always finds a way to find the light, your light. You see, your experience and analysis of the relationship may not line up with others. At some point, you have to put your own label on it, but yours will be based on how you have come to view them, your truths about the individual. Sometimes the truth is that this person might not be someone that you need in your life as much as they need you in theirs. God might be bringing you two together for a specific reason. Caution! You can't let your openness be a call to try and save the world, no one person can. However, there could be opportunities to save or make a difference in some people's lives.

In 2011, Renee's family reunion came to Ohio, Youngstown

to be specific. Renee is my current wife. A reunion committee was formed, and we proceeded to make it happen. Renee was elected chairperson. The reunion moniker is "Where there is love, there is unity." However, a disturbing thing started to surface during the planning phase of what was to be a three-day weekend celebration of family.

The more we strived toward putting the pieces together and getting others involved with the process, the less "Love and unity," we felt. So, I decided to try and fix some of that with a challenge to the family at the banquet on Sunday, the last day of the reunion. I asked the committee for a ten-minute slot on the program. I was also Master of Ceremonies for the event. My request was granted with one provision from Renee, "Don't get up there and act silly." I have sometimes been known to poke fun at people and things. Anyway, I agreed to keep it civil.

I told no one of my subject matter, I simply told them to put my name in the program with the topic of D.A.S.H. This was my attempt at being clever. Making this look like an anagram for something, would not give away what I would be speaking on. When it was my turn on the program, I first informed them that the D.A.S.H. was not an anagram for anything but rather, just the word dash. I further explained that it represented that horizontal line you see on the headstones in cemeteries that separates a person's birth and death dates, representing their entire life.

I then talked about the overwhelming experience I had at my family's reunion earlier in the year, and why. I explained that we always have tables setup with pictures of all the family members that had died. For the first time, for some reason, I spent a lot of time there in reflection. I was reflecting on the impact, if any, each person had on my life. There were some that I respectfully acknowledged and quickly moved on, while with others I stopped and reflected for a long time with a thankful and grateful heart.

These were the people that spent valuable time with me and helped to shape the person that I have become. They poured into me and caused me to love and respect them. Not just for telling me that they loved me, but for showing me how much they loved me and cared about my well-being and future. They were my GPS and headlights during good times and when things were dark for me. They help to guide me through my life's journeys.

The time spent at those tables had an impact on me and caused me to ask some hard questions to myself. The hardest was, "Whose life am I impacting?" The follow-up was, "Why or why not?" I did a lot of soul searching in the days that followed. That set the table for what I really wanted to talk about.

I asked a question. "When your picture arrives on some table, how many of your family members will simply acknowledge you and quickly walk by, and how many will stop, reflect, and be eternally grateful for what you meant to them in their life?" I gave them a moment to let those words take root, then I issued the challenge.

I first told them about something I had started doing with my great nephew and grandson, they were twelve and eleven. Every three weeks we would go to the public library, and each of us would return and check out a book of our own choosing. Then we would go to lunch. The choice of where we went would rotate between the three of us; no eatery was off limits. Lucky for me, they mostly liked junk food. We would go to the nicer restaurants when it was my turn to pick. During lunch, we would engage in conversation about the books we read over the previous three weeks and some light-hearted life stuff. It was a fun few hours on a Saturday afternoon.

I explained to the family members that I was trying to build a relationship with them beyond my title of uncle and grandpa. My hopes were that our bond over the coming years would be strong enough, respectful enough, and loving enough for them to be comfortable coming to me if they ever needed help. Help in sorting out some of the life size issues, I knew that could possibly be coming their way some day.

I acknowledged that I felt the room was filled with good family members that would help out if they could, if someone in the family reached out to them. Then I presented the challenge. I said, rather than waiting for someone to reach out in what might be an emergency, be intentional about helping someone. I asked them to emotionally adopt some of the younger family members and start to pour into them. That could take many different forms, there are a lot of ways to let young people know how much you care about them.

I didn't leave the challenge there; I also mentioned the senior family members with all the possible situations they might be facing. I encouraged those that could, to reach out to them as well to help brighten some of their remaining days. My last point was to remind everyone that everything does not have to be tied to money. That sometimes, a giving of someone's time can actually be more valuable. Sometime, people just need someone to listen to what they have to say or to talk to them. I received some positive feedback and was hopeful that my efforts might drive some helpful family interactions.

THE GOLF TOURNAMENT

I believe the love and pull associated with family and friends are the strongest emotions in the world. They have the ability to make the good times better and the bad ones tolerable.

I once went to a professional golf tournament at the Firestone Country Club in Akron, Ohio. This was my first tournament, and I was excited to see some of my favorite golfers. Back then, it was Tiger Woods, Payne Stewart, and Freddie "Boom-Boom" Couples. I couldn't interest anyone into coming with me, so I went alone.

I was standing around one of the greens watching the players come through, this hole was a par four. Payne Stewart had teed off and his ball ended up in the rough on the right side of the fairway. When he got to his ball, he called for the rules official. His ball was sitting in a bad spot, and he was hoping that he would get some relief. He was denied, he had to play it where it was sitting. His ball was in the rough about 180 yards away at a bad angle to the hole on the green. This would be a very difficult shot to get close to the target. He lines up, hits the ball and it ends up about four feet from the hole. All of us around the green go crazy; it was a spectacular shot! People are clapping, high- fiving their friends, and screaming. I'm one of the clappers looking to my left then right, wanting to express myself further and I was surrounded by strangers.

I made myself a promise that day and I've kept it. I said that I would never attend another golf tournament alone. That brilliant moment was somewhat tarnished because I had no one to share it with.

I wanted to talk about family because it touches so many facets of our lives. Family and friends are who we identify with and ultimately is the major source of our lasting memories, good and bad. The people closest to us are the ones we love the most but also hold the power to hurt us the most.

My mother and grandmother both died in nursing homes. I was blessed to be retired when they went in. This allowed me to visit every day when I wasn't out of town, and I did. Some days would be better than others for me, but they were all emotional. There were many days that I sat in the parking lot after a visit, fighting back tears. In those moments, I was not thinking about how much money I did or didn't have, I was not focused on the type or brand of car I was driving. Fighting back those tears didn't give me cause to think about my neighborhood or how big my house was. Those moments were reminders of what was really important to me, my family, and friends.

There's an industry that's been built up and in place called Treasure Hunters. Most of their searches are in bodies of water. Their research tells them what the treasures are, they just don't know exactly where. When they go out searching, they are focused because they know the potential value of what they seek.

I know that I've talked and shared a lot about "Family

Mess" stuff. However, I believe there is much more surrounding family and friends that is healthy and good. Stuff has always happened, and it always will. One of the things that I have come to realize, is that no matter what happens in life, there is always a decision to be made for what is "NEXT." If our next is following something positive, then we will try to build on that. If it follows something negative, we try to fix it, this is true most of the time. One of the things we sometimes struggle with is identifying what is good or bad for us. That can cause us to make decisions that can lead to "**Family Mess**."

I believe that some of our life's decisions become easier when we have a clear vision and understanding as to what we treasure and focus on in decision making circumstances. I also believe in most cases that family and friends are valuable treasures worth searching and fighting for.

CHAPTER 7

-MONEY; FRIEND OR FOE?

Money is a necessary tool for living.
Some tools come with safety cautions,
money should be one of them.

When our son Kevin was between the ages of seven and eight, something happened to him. He seemingly overnight became obsessed with money. His obsession became very noticeable, concerning, and sometimes annoying. At some point I was starting to get embarrassed from wondering about what other people thought was going on within our home. Did they think that we were broke, didn't have enough food to eat, or perhaps we had decorated with and were sitting on orange crates?

It was at that point I decided to address the issue with him. It was summer, he was outside playing, and I had a couple of hours before I had to leave for work. I called him in and asked him to join me at the kitchen table because I wanted to have a money talk. We're seated, and I begin with my concerns about his non-stop talking about money. Thinking back, my first question probably should have been, "Why?" but it wasn't. My first question and his first answer was the beginning and ending of our impromptu meeting.

My question was, "Kevin, you do realize that money won't make you happy?"

His reply, "But Dad, you can't do anything without it!" He didn't hesitate, didn't think about it, didn't bat-an-eye. His response almost started before I had completed the question. It was like he had this money thing figured out and there was nothing to think about. I was so surprised by his quick response and answer, I just told him to go back outside. I didn't have a good comeback because he was right, and I had taken my well thought-out best shot.

I decided to keep an eye on his money attitude and see how it would develop and play out. It turned out not to be a bad thing and his family today is doing very well financially. Many years later, after he was an adult, I did get around to asking the "why" question and this is what I found out. He had gone to the grocery store with a neighborhood friend and his mother. As they were walking the aisles, his friend was asking for brand named things. Each time he did, his mother was saying "no," that they couldn't afford it and pointed him to the generic brands. That was his turning point and awakening to the importance and power of money.

Living life comes with its situations and complications which drives emotions. There's not a family in the world that has not been impacted by the ups and downs of having to manage some of those outcomes. My family, when I was growing up was no different. There are times when we look back on some of that history and wonder what happened. Truth is that life was happening and often times being shaped by our decisions. In those moments, it will be clear that at some of those times money was just along for the ride, but at other times money was doing the driving; some may have been reckless.

I think that we all can agree that money plays a major role in our lives. The delta gets to be how we feel about it, how we go after it, and what we choose to do with it after it's in our hands. The feel part can range from worship to a means to an end. How we try to get it and how we use it is also endless and personal.

Everybody makes money plans because money drives lifestyles and lifestyle plans. How we live, where we live, and our plans for future living is driven by the money we have and our plans around future income. Planning one's future shows responsibility. There are good plans, not so good plans, bad plans, illogical plans, irresponsible plans, and the list goes on. Some plans are pulled off without a hitch, while others have to be adjusted and still others abandoned; complete start-overs.

Most plans require some level of work, sacrifice, and dedication. Some require more than others, like years of education pursuing a dream and the associated lifestyle. Some are willing to put in that kind of time and work, while others want the quick fix. Our prison systems are filled with the quick fixers.

The end result of money plans doesn't necessarily reflect intelligence. Some of the smartest people in the world have criminal records. Most of the time, our lifestyles are more a reflection of choice than how smart we are. What we do may not be who we are. Doing something dumb doesn't mean that you're stupid. Smart people do dumb things all the time. We have to understand that an act that is done may not accurately represent the person that committed the act. Even really bad people sometimes do good things. What I'm really saying is that who we are at our core, may not consistently represent our actions.

The norm of society is constantly putting us or more accurately dividing us into categories. Bad people do bad things; good people do good things. However, we know that kind of thinking can be a false narrative. Money and society's take on it does the same thing. Society says that money paints a type of picture of us and tries to label who we are. To some degree, that's right. You're typically not going to see someone in the middle to lower income bracket driving around in a new Rolls-Royce. If you do, they either stole it or are chauffeuring the owner.

Two weeks after I changed jobs, where I worked, a co-worker approached me with a directive. He said now that I was going to be making more money, I needed to start looking for a house in a better neighborhood. At that time, he was also the president of the local credit union. He didn't know much about me. He certainly didn't know my lifestyle or where I lived. To him it didn't matter, more money, better standard of living. He equated that to real estate. He didn't suggest a better car or more expensive clothing. His idea of upgrading my standard of living that this additional money was going to provide, was to upgrade my neighborhood. You see, the job upgrade was when I went into Tool and Die. Perhaps he was saying, now that I have a White job, making White money, I ought to move out of the Hood!

When you start to handle more money, some things in your life should change. However, those "things" are what we as individuals should decide on our own based on our values, not societies. The key to that is knowing and not being afraid to be who you are.

We constantly see problems at every income level with people trying to please or live up to the societal norms. Average people buying things they really can't afford, pushing up their debt level. Rich people living in gated communities, driving certain types of cars, being invited to all the right events while perhaps behind closed doors are hiding their true values and living a life of misery. Your financial echelon means very little when stacked against what you really value and who you really are.

Money is no different than anything else we are emotional about. Mistreating or misusing it can cause major problems in our lives. Yes, I believe there is an emotional attachment to our connection with money. The level of attachment is what drives a lot of our decisions. I see this as no different than our approach to personal relationships; it's emotional.

Money, or the pursuit of it, can make us feel happy, sad (like you're in love with it), or depressed (like you've just climbed to the top of Mount Everest, or perhaps fallen into a deep dark hole with no easy way out). That just scratches the surface of the types of holds that money can put on us. I see money as a tool, the right tool for the right job makes the work easier. Being careless with tools can cause serious personal injuries, being careless with money can cause serious personal problems.

In this chapter I will not be offering advice as to what to do with your money. I'm actually the last person anyone should seek financial advice from. I lost over $70,000 in a three-month period in 2008, in the stock market. Talk to someone else about investments. However, I will share this concerning the stock market, buy low, sell high, and don't try to time the market; basic 101 market stuff. That's all I've got. The balance of my financial knowledge is this; keep a close eye on your credit rating. That is very important to everyone's financial being. I've been told that I have Rock Star credit; I worked hard to get it.

We all have money stories as to how, and perhaps why we've gotten as far as we have. Likewise, we all have stories of our money triumphs, missteps, and lessons learned during the pursuits of financial endeavors. In this chapter, I'll simply be sharing some of mine.

THE NEIGHBORHOODS

When I was discharged from the military in January 1970, my wife and son were living with her parents on the North Side of Youngstown. I moved in and we stayed there for about a year to help save for our first home. Her mother was a classy, hard-working lady that I came to love and respect very much. Her father was quite a character. I liked him, and we always got along. His nickname for our son was "The Bandit." His game was checkers. We played many-a-games, and his record remains perfect; I was never able to beat him.

I got the advice from someone in the tool room, to move to a better neighborhood in 1972. We actually did move in 1985. Our move wasn't based on looking for a better location as much as it was about getting away from the one we were in. Wanting to leave our neighborhood of fourteen years was based on a series of events.

March 17, 1971, we moved into the neighborhood, it was our first house. It was on the East Side of town in an area called Lincoln Knolls. This was not far from the Sharon Line area where I grew up. It was a development of moderate but nice three-bedroom homes, most had full basements. There were three basic designs scattered throughout. We had remodeled most of the house, especially the basement and all of the outside landscaping. It had become very comfortable for us, and we loved it.

The neighborhood started to change as a result of the infamous closings of some steel mills that came to be known as "Black Monday." This actually happened September 19, 1977. It was a big blow for the Youngstown area and hit our neighborhood pretty hard. It was six years after we had moved in. Our neighbors on both sides of us and directly across the street, worked in the mills and lost their jobs because of the closings. Our neighbors on the right of us were Puerto Rican. A few years after losing his job, he moved with his family back to Puerto Rico. They were nice people and good neighbors. I was sad to see them leave.

One Saturday night, about 2:00 a.m., we were introduced to our new neighbors. Our bedroom, my wife, and I were on the driveway side of their house. We were awakened with a loud bang, which turned out to be the "For Sale" sign being thrown against their house. That was followed with a loud, drunken declaration of, "This motherf...... house is mine."

The neighbors across the street, who were also friends, wound up getting a divorce. Our neighbor on the left, turned into a non-stop doom & gloom, the sky- is-falling type of person. Every negative thing that he read in the papers, local and abroad, I was getting warned that it was coming our way. The neighborhood was taking on a different feel, none of that felt good but things would get worse.

Our house was broken into, and we didn't know it at first. We found out one-night ordering pizza for dinner. It was Friday and I didn't cash my paycheck for some reason. We always kept some cash in the house for minor emergencies. I went to get some for the pizza, and it was gone. I asked the wife if she had taken it and she said, "No." After a few minutes of "what the hell happened," we started noticing some other things missing. Things like some of my wife's underwear and lingerie pieces, there were also a few pictures missing. We didn't call the police; we just changed all the locks on the doors. We remembered that our son had lost his key playing outside. We figured that someone found it and decided to make themselves at home in our house. When someone has broken into your home, the house takes on a different feel; uncomfortable.

The last and final straw came in the summer of 1985. Some neighborhood teenagers had gathered across the street in the front yard to the right of the neighbors that divorced. It's the middle of the week and weeks before the 4th of July. They are lighting and throwing "firecrackers" for hours. It's sneaking up on 11:00 p.m., I have to go to work in the morning and I've heard enough. I marched over, told them about the legality of what they were doing, the fact that I had to work in the morning, and the fact that I was tired of hearing the fireworks. They were silent. I walked back across the street. I'm halfway up my driveway when someone lit a firecracker and launched it into the street. I stopped dead in my tracks and stood there with my back to them for about five minutes, just waiting and fuming. There were no more firecrackers, so I went back inside the house. When I got to my wife, I announced, "We were moving!"

I told her what happened because she didn't know I had left the house. I explained the foolishness of what I was just contemplating and said again, "It's time to go." She didn't push back because she preferred to live on her side of town growing up anyway, the North Side.

There is a part of the North Side that is made up of large stately homes. It's now identified as the "Historical District;" we moved a few blocks away. Our house is on a street that is two blocks long. The block that we're on has some colorful history. It got even more colorful when we moved in because we were the first Blacks to purchase a house on the street. I was the first Black in the Tool and Die apprentice program and now our family has that same distinction here.

There's a book written by Allen R. May and published in 2013 titled, "*Crimetown U.S.A. The history of the Mahoning Valley Mafia, Organized Crime Activity in Ohio's Steel Valley; 1933 – 1963.*" There's a chapter in the book titled, "*The Policy Kings.*" Most of this chapter is focused on the crime activity of the Naples brothers, primarily Sandy. They were part of the Pittsburgh Mafia. Two of the brother's homes are pictured in the book. They are both on the block that we moved into.

Our house is the third from the corner. When we first moved there, the corner house was owned by William "Billy" Naples. His widow was living there. The second next to ours, was owned by Anthony B. Flask, a former mayor of Youngstown. His widow was living there alone. On the same side of the street, seven houses up, lived "Joey" Naples with his wife and German Shepherd dog. Joey was Capo of the Youngstown faction. Joey was killed by a high-powered rifle August 19, 1991; six years after we moved in. His brother Billy was killed in his car by a bomb July 1, 1962. His oldest brother Sandy was murdered on March 11, 1960, with a shotgun at his girlfriend's house.

Joey was the youngest of four brothers. He used to walk his dog in the early evening hours, sometimes with his wife. If I was in the yard, he would always speak. The first time we came close to a conversation, I was up in a tree in the front yard trimming some branches with a small hand bow saw. He stopped on the sidewalk and told me that it looked nice and that I probably should stop. My first thought was, "You take care of your place up the street, I can handle this." What I actually said was something like this, "I was just about to come down to see how it was looking, thanks." He always dressed nice, and I liked him. Before we moved in, he probably knew more about me than I did. He was dangerous but pretty cool.

Directly across the street from us lived Dom Rosselli and his wife. He was the legendary men's basketball coach for Youngstown State University. He coached basketball for 38 years, baseball coach for 31 years, and assistant football coach for more than 20 years. He retired in 1982, three years before we moved in. He and his wife were the first to welcome us to the neighborhood. That warm welcome wagon didn't extend to my neighbor on the left, the ex- mayor's house. A few weeks after we moved in, a very nice wooden privacy fence was installed around the back yard.

Coming home from work one day, I walked in from the garage and one of the dining room windows exploded. We had been in the house about two months. I immediately hit the floor because I thought that it had been shot out. After a few seconds, I crawled over to the bank of windows, peaked out and saw our son standing in the back yard holding one of my golf clubs. He had a strange look on his face. He was constantly looking down at the ground and back up at the hole in the window. I was instantly relieved to know that it was a golf ball and not a bullet. On that crawl over to the windows, I was thinking the worse. I have been living here over thirty years now and the fence was the worst of it. We now have a second Mayor of Youngstown living on our block, Jamael Tito Brown.

What IF?

Somewhere, in my senior year of high school, I made the decision that I would not pursue a college degree. I worked hard in school and got good grades, but I had a problem that only me and my mother knew about. It was my eyes. I started wearing glasses when I was in the third grade. The optometrist said that my glasses should be the last thing I take off at night and the first thing I put on when I get out of bed in the morning. He said that I was nearsighted and farsighted with astigmatic eyes. I had a hard time reading or studying longer than two hours. After that, I would develop an eye ache which actually felt like a headache. The longer I went past two hours, the worse the ache.

One of my teachers that year gave me a preview of what college life could be like. He painted a picture of meeting different people and having fun, but he really talked up the hard work part of it, reading and studying. He said that it was like high school but more intense. He explained that none of the professors would care about how much work your other professors were demanding, they only cared about theirs. He went on to say that the workload could get pretty heavy at times, especially during finals. That was very worrisome for me because of my eye-studying issues. I was starting to view college as a four-year, non-stop headache. The more I thought about it, the more I didn't want to put myself through that; high school was bad enough.

I started trying to picture my future without college. I felt that I was smart and knew that I was a hard worker. I grew up surrounded by hard working adults and they made it, I knew that I could, too. My decision to forgo college was very disappointing to some members of my family, especially my mother and grandmother. My mother knew my condition and understood. My grandmother always saw big things in my future, perhaps as a doctor but no college meant that was off the table. She still had high hopes for me. There were offers inside and outside of the family to help with financing college and let me know that they saw something special in me. However, my mind was made up, no college, I would find another way.

The Sixties offered a variety of ways to make money, all legal. There were a lot of good-paying jobs with benefits in the manufacturing fields, I figured that I could land one of them. I was fortunate and blessed that I did, and things worked out for me and my family.

Time always drives change. The landscape of opportunities for good jobs, without some college or technical training has changed dramatically, especially in the manufacturing arenas. The advancements in artificial intelligence (AI) and robotics has been a game changer and job eliminator. You could be a person with outstanding, hard work ethics and find it difficult to make it in the 2000s without some formal training or education past high school.

I sometimes do what most people do from time to time, play the "what if" game. If I had done this or that, if I had married this person or the other, how would my life have turned out. I have asked that question of myself concerning college many-a-times. With my work ethic and a college degree on my resume, what would Fred Stringer look like today? Who knows. I try not to visit that "what if" question too often. I see no positivity in it when applied to the past; fruitless. However, applied to our futures, the positive possibilities are endless; they are called dreams. This is still why we work hard and do some of the things that we do.

Some of the "what if" drive and anticipation is good, others, not so much. Some of the others are things like playing the lottery and straight hard-core gambling. We have all seen some negative family results from going down those type roads. "What if" I change the subject now; I think I will.

THINGS I LEARNED ABOUT MONEY
BEFORE THE 6TH GRADE

MONEY	
Working for it	*GOOD*
Extortion	*BAD*
Saving for a rainy day	*SMART*
Throwing it away	*DUMB*

Growing up, there was a lady that lived three houses up from us on the same side of the street, named Mrs. Douglas. She was very good friends with my grandmother. She and my grandmother were also part of the same garden club. Mrs. Douglas had a lot of yard, front, back, and side that had flower beds and other shrubs that needed maintaining; that's where I came in. Helping her with the yard work was my first regular-paying summer job. I was about nine years old. It was a five day-a-week job but only a few hours per day. I was paid with a 5-dollar bill each Friday.

Pay day was always a good feeling. I knew that I had worked hard so it never felt like a gift, I felt that I had earned it. What was even a better feeling was sharing some of that with my mother. She would never take much, most times she would take nothing, but it made me feel good to offer.

Saving was never big on my radar unless I was working on a special project, which was rare. I once saved for an engine for a metal go-cart that I planned to one day build, it never happened. I did get the engine, but you can't ride an engine. Another "what if" dream shattered! The reason I had a metal go-cart on my mind was because my neighbor Lewis helped me build one out of 2 X 4s once. I would charge the neighborhood kids five cents to ride on it. The front wheels were attached to a 2 X 4 and a rope was also attached. Between that being a bad design and me being tired of pushing my customers, that money venture lasted about one week.

I took another shot at making some money one summer; I was about ten. We had three neighborhood small stores within walking distance and a public park, Bailey, at the end of our street. This big idea was to open a candy stand on the sidewalk in front of my grandmother's house. This put my candy between the park and the first store. I built the stand and only sold penny candy. I would buy two pieces for a penny and sell it for a penny a-piece. I saved the kids a few steps while I was making a handy profit. Things were going good until my candy source found out what I was doing.

I went in to replenish my stock and the owner proceeded to explain why I needed to close my new enterprise. It wasn't a long conversation with a lot of details, he simply said that I didn't have a license to do what I was doing and if I didn't stop, he would call the police. Hey, I was 10, it sounded kind of scary; it was time to move on. Another summer venture that lasted about a week. Between Mrs. Douglas, my go-cart, and candy businesses, I was starting to understand the relationship with hard work and money.....*GOOD*

During my summer break between the 4th and 5th grades, I tried my hand at being a gangster, kind of. Me and a friend we called Rabbit devised a scheme to take money from this kid called Shae Bay that lived with his grandmother in Hubbard. Hubbard was a city only one street over from the street that I lived on. It was mostly my idea; Rabbit just went along with it.

It wasn't a long, thought-out, elaborate plan, it just happened one day when Rabbit and I ran into Shae Bay at Bailey Park, and we started talking. During the conversation, we found out some things that were going on with him. Things like he would get money from his grandmother once -a-month things like he would give some of that money to some boys in Hubbard once-a-month. He let us know that he wasn't happy with that arrangement. He also let us know that he had just gotten the money and that the Hubbard boys would probably be looking for him within a couple of days.

This was the plan, I suggested that he give me and Rabbit some money that was less than what they were taking from him and not pay the Hubbard boys. That way he would have more of his money to keep for himself. To make the plan work, he was to tell them that he had given their money to me and Rabbit and that he didn't have anymore. We settled on $10.00; Rabbit and I both got a 5-dollar bill. Shae Bay was happy while Rabbit and I could hardly believe our good fortune.

As we walked home from the park, we thought that we had gotten away with something pretty cool. However, it turned out to be anything but. Our plan worked out about as smooth and seamless as someone robbing a bank with a class reunion name tag pinned to their jacket; it didn't go very well. Two days after we got the money, Rabbit ran down to my house breathing heavy and bearing bad news. He had just left the park, where he had just been confronted by some boys looking for Shae Bay's money. I asked how many were there and what did he do? He said a lot, and that he gave up the five bucks. I asked why did he give up the money? He replied, "So I wouldn't get beat up." He then said that this was a heads up because they were coming for me next.

Great! So now my two-man gangster squad has been narrowed down to one, me, and I'm not feeling very tough after that report. The reason Rabbit was out of breath was because he ran down to my house to warn me of my now pending future.

Rabbit got off easy, he still had the $5.00 to return. How he was able to hang on to that money for two days is still a mystery to me. My fate however, was starting to look a lot different than his; all my money was gone. I did a lot of walking to the corner stores in those two days, and now I'm broke. At first, I was disappointed with Rabbit because I knew that the Hubbard boys would come looking for us eventually. I didn't know that, in Rabbit's words, it would be "a lot." I figured two, maybe three at the most. My plan was to talk some "scary tough guy shit" to them and get them to back down or worse case, just fight them.

We're still in the front yard when Rabbit looks up the street and says, "Here they come, "and takes off toward his house. I look up and see what appears to be a mob of blackness coming my way. My first thought was damn, was he paying off the whole neighborhood? Then I did what any want-to-be tough guy would do facing that situation, I ran into our garage and hid. It turns out that I wasn't that tough, but I definitely wasn't that stupid either.

Our garage had an apartment over it. I knew where the key was kept because I had to clean it once a month. My father was part of a men's club called "The Gaylords" and this is where they held their monthly meetings. Now, I'm inside peeping out of the front window which has the view of the back of our house and the driveway. I see these guys, with Shae Bay in the middle, cross the driveway and approach our front door. This is more trouble for me because I know my mother is inside. After a few minutes, I see them cross the driveway again heading back in the direction of the park.

It wasn't long after that, I hear my mother calling my name in the front yard and it didn't sound like she was very happy. Now, I have only two choices; come out now or wait 'til later.

My only options are the timing, because either way I'm going to get a whipping that I will remember for a few days.

My mother paid the five dollars, whipped my butt and this was added to the list of things she didn't think that I would ever do. At the same time, gangster was taken off my list of things I wanted to do going forward. I figured that there were safer ways to make money, something other than dealing with the police and gang violence.

I waited a couple of days before I went back to the park. There was no drama with the Hubbard gang. They just wanted the money, and they made sure that Shae Bay didn't make that mistake again.

Extortion…..*BAD*

Growing up, I can only remember my father giving me two pieces of advice.

1. "If you're not spending your money, you're not using it right."

2. "Don't trust anybody, not even your own father."

That second piece came while I was helping him work on a fence project. He was pounding a tall U-shaped metal pole, with notches for stringing wire, into the ground. He was on a ladder with a sledgehammer while I was on the ground holding it steady with my hands near the top. On one swing, he missed the pole and came down on my hands. Thus, "don't trust anybody …" That advice actually had more merit than #1. If I had money saved up, I could have paid Shae Bay back and avoided a good whipping.

Saving for a rainy day…..*SMART*

During those early years, I developed an odd relationship with the 5-dollar bill. Mrs. Douglas paid me with a 5; I extorted a 5, and then one day, I found a 5-dollar bill lying in the middle of the street. Looking back, perhaps if it had been any other denomination but the 5, the outcome might have been different.

I had gone over a friend's house several streets from mine to hang out. On the way back home toward the end of his street, a 5-dollar bill was lying there. I remember picking it up and thinking that this was an opportunity to do something good. I turned around and started walking back up the street. I knocked on the door of the first house I came to and asked if they had lost 5 dollars? It was a woman that answered the door, she said, "No," and closed the door. I proceeded to the next house. A man answered the door. I asked the same question. He looked over my head, then up and down the street, paused, then said "Yea." I handed him the 5, he said thanks; I had one good deed in the books.

I could hardly wait 'til I got home to tell the story to my mother. However, I didn't get the "good for you, I'm proud of you," response that I was anticipating, it was quite the opposite. She gave me one of those "you did what" looks. I'll spare you the rest of the conversation, but I can tell you, I came away feeling anything but smart.

Throwing money away.....*DUMB*

FIRST REAL JOBS

My first job out of high school was at the Republic Steel Mill Center Street Division in Youngstown, Ohio. In 1965, the steel mills were on the decline but still played a major role in the economy of Youngstown. I had been working there about three months when I got laid off two times in one week. I decided that the mill's future for a young man was somewhere between dim and dark. That decision drove a conversation with my grandmother.

At that time, she was a practical nurse at one of the largest hospitals in Youngstown, St. Elizabeth on the North Side of town. She said that she would work her magic and get me a job there, and she did. In the late 1950s, my mother also worked there for a few years in the laundry department. My job title was, "*Inhalation Specialist*" nice title, not so nice pay. I had a high school friend, Gilliam, that was already working there in the kitchen department. He and some co-workers would meet in a small room for lunch, and I got to be part of that group.

Occasionally, Doug would sneak in a pie from the kitchen.

I remember opening my first paycheck during lunch with the fellas. Everybody in the room was pissed off after I revealed it. I was pissed because it was way less than what I had been making at the steel mill. They were pissed because it was more than they were making, and I had just gotten there. They were working in housekeeping and the kitchen.

One of my lasting memories from that job was getting the first true love of my life, my first car stolen from the parking lot. It was a 1960 two door Impala, white with a red strip on the sides, red interior, custom taillights, "Baby Moon" hub caps, and clean enough to eat off the floors. I told the security guard that I couldn't find my car and he said, "Oh, your car's been stolen?" At that point, everything started moving in slow motion except my heart, it started to race. I knew my car wasn't where I had left it, but I couldn't bring myself to use the word "stolen." I remember feeling like I was five years old again, about to cry over something I couldn't control. I was a long way away from five and never wanted to feel that way again.

It was New Year's Eve, and I had a date with my first wife. I was also starting a new job at Packard Electric in January. No car for my date, no car to start my new job. My 1966 beginning was pretty shaky. I wasn't feeling very happy for the "New Year." That incident changed my attitude about my future cars. I still like nice cars and take good care of them, but there are no more love affairs. I see cars now as a means to an end, transportation. Now, I reserve my love for things with a heartbeat and a pulse.

38 YEAR CAREER AT PACKARD ELECTRIC / DELPHI

It's the tail-end of November 1965. Packard Electric has placed ads in several newspapers and other medias that they would be hiring and taking applications on a certain date to fill a variety of positions. That was all that was needed to create a line around the building, camp out all night, cattle-call of anticipations for a job. Packard had always been a cherished job, and most people felt that way.

That announcement hiring was targeted to start accepting applications early on a Saturday morning. At this particular time, I'm fresh out of high school, living at home, and working at St. Elizabeth hospital. The military is also looming very near in my future. My mother and her sister, Aunt Maggie, wanted to apply for one of those jobs. They also want me to drive them there and be with them all night to help save their place in line. Two would stay in line while one would go back to the car to get warm.

I hadn't planned on applying for a job because I knew that I would be going to the military soon. However, when the doors were finally opened, I happened to be in line, so I went in. As fate would have it, we all applied but I was the only one hired; the one that didn't really want a job. It was a better paying job than the one I had, so I gave notice to the hospital and started at Packard, January 10, 1966. That was the beginning of a career that ended with retirement on January 1, 2004, 38 years later.

There was a probation period of 90 days that had to be satisfied to become a permanent, full-time employee. I didn't have my 90 days in when rumors started to circulate that there were going to be layoffs. In most industries, with hourly workers, seniority is king; last ones in, first to be let go. The foreman that I worked for knew that I would not have my time in when the layoffs were scheduled to hit his department. He liked how I worked and wanted me to get my probation time in. He made arrangements for me to be transferred to a department that still had full work schedules. He was hoping that I could last there long enough to get my 90 days in. His plan worked. I did get laid off but not before I got through my probation period, I made it by twelve days.

I was laid off in April and started in the Air Force June 21, 1966. When it was time for me to enlist, I was still living at home. I owe my entire Packard career to the wisdom of my mother. Because I was still laid off in June, I was simply going to leave for the military and not notify Packard of my mandatory obligation to the Air Force. My mother sat me down to explain some things about the future. She said that no one could possibly know what kind of shape the country would be in when my four years would conclude in the Air Force. She insisted that I go up to Packard and fill out the military leave paperwork. Her advice to me that day proved to be very wise counsel. When I came back, the economy was not doing good and many industries were struggling, including Packard, they had many people laid off.

Packard had done very well during the four years that I was away. They had built several new plants and hired hundreds of new people. Because I had filed military papers, all my time in the military counted toward my seniority. When I got back, I had over four years on the books. That gave me more seniority than over half the people working there. That presented the possibility that one more person would be laid off to make room for me. I was married now with a baby boy and thankful to have a job. I was also determined to take full advantage of the opportunity my mother had secured for me and my new family.

Very few working careers are non-stop smooth sailing, it is

seldom going to be all good or all bad. Another truth is that there will always be people trying to lift you up and others, perhaps for the same reasons, trying to tear/break you down. There could also be times for difficult work-related decisions along the way. I had some help with managing the pressures of tough decisions in my career, but it came at a tremendous price.

When my wife died, I was a supervisor in engineering. Her death started to tint the lens I looked at the world through, concerning certain things. One of those things was my approach to problems at work specifically, and at life generally. Her death gave me clear definition between a problem and a crisis. Life and death issues are crisis, everything else is just problem-solving. In my mind, losing my wife and all that came with it, while having a child in high school and another in college, was a crisis. For me, everything else fail short of that. From that point, until I retired, whatever the immediacy around a set of decisions and directions that some were calling a crisis, were merely problem-solving situations to me. It helped to keep my blood pressure down and my mind clear.

When you retire out of engineering, you are presented with a plaque that is designed to look like a patent award. I do have a Patent and Trade Secret plaques on a shelf in our office, I made room for this one to join them. This plaque offered congratulations and listed the jobs I held over my 38 years. I remember thinking that it didn't seem right that all those years could be held in my hands. Truth is, sometimes when you look backward, most things can seem short and small.

This is what my career patent looks like	
01-1966	*New Hire – Service General*
06-1966	*Air Force – Military Leave*
01-1970	*Service General*
02-1971	*General Labor*
03-1972	*Tool and Die*
02-1979	*Tool Engineering – Assembly Dies*
06-1981	*Tool Engineering – Injection Molds*
01-1984	*Project Engineering – Component Design; Divisional Manufacturing Engineering*
06-1985	*Administrator, Speed-O-Matic Crib*
07-1986	*Administrator, Speed-O-Matic Crib and Grinnell Warehouse*
07-1987	*Administrator, Speed-O-Matic Crib and Divisional Die Group*
03-1989	*Supervisor, Speed-O-Matic Crib and Divisional Die Group*
06-1998	*Supervisor, Assembly Die Design and Build Group*
01-2004	*Retired*

The Speed-O-Matic Crib was a fun job. It was a separate run business within the Packard company. It was an office/warehouse of presses, dies, and component parts that we sold to small production shops that supported and sold Packard finished products. We were totally independent and responsible for our budget, staff, and inventory. The fun for me was learning how to run a business and working with our staff. There were only five of us and it felt like a family. We had a sound system (radio), that was on all day. I learned to appreciate and like some Country music. I would sometimes come home singing songs that my wife and kids had never heard before, they would look at me funny. Great job, and I learned a lot, but other challenges were in my future.

One of the highlights of my career was getting to know and work with a lot of nice people. Another one worth mentioning is the travel opportunities I was afforded: Mexico, Germany, Austria, Spain, Italy, Portugal, and Brazil. My current wife is from the town of Warren, Ohio. Packard was founded and headquartered there. I sometimes tease her that Warren should be added to my passport and that she owes me for rescuing her from that strange country, she never laughs!

Some of my lasting memories and certainly on my highlight page was the involvement I had with mentoring some of the people that crossed my path. I was part of a formal mentoring program associated with a group that was sanctioned by Packard. The group was, "The Black Outreach Network at Packard," (B.O.N.D.). These were young Black men and women, newly hired and fresh out of college.

B.O.N.D. was structured and you were assigned a mentee, that was interesting and sometimes presented a unique challenge. There were other types of mentoring that I also enjoyed. That's when people Black and White would seek me out for advice. It was rewarding to help and gratifying to know that people thought enough of me to want to pick my brain and experience for possible direction.

I need to mention one low-light because it served as a wake-up call and helped to shape my mental bearing during most of my career at Packard. I call it my "Green Grinding Wheel Experience."

THE GREEN GRINDING WHEEL

To become a journeyman Tool and Die Maker, you must complete the apprenticeship program. The program is very regimented. It spells out the number of classroom hours to be completed and the subjects to be covered, mostly math and mechanical theories. It also determines the number of hours you must spend on each piece of machinery/tooling under journeyman supervision. The program generally takes four years.

There were a lot of things I had to learn on my way to becoming a card-carrying journeyman. Most of what I learned was dictated by the conditions and guidelines of the apprenticeship program itself. While this proved to be a non-stop process of learning the trade, there was one lesson I learned one night that was personal to me only. This was something that took me by surprise and has stayed with me to this very day.

At the time this happened, I had been in the program for about three years. This program or class of new apprentice was unique to the company. It was the first time they brought on 24 at one time; I was the only Black. Up until that point, new apprentice starts would typically be one-to-three at a time. There seemed to be a fair amount of nepotism and politics surrounding the selections. Because this was a special class, special measures were put in place to handle such a large number. The most notable change was the construction of a new tool room. The company created the "Apprentice Tool Room" and equipped it with the machines that represented the standard tool rooms only at a smaller scale.

Another change for the class was that we would spend the first year of our training in this tool room setting. Normally, a new apprentice would be assigned to one of the many tool rooms located in the various departments throughout the different plants. The company felt that the transition to the regular tool rooms would be a lot easier for us because of the year we had working with the machinery.

Like I said, I was in the program for about three years but only in my assigned tool room for two. The prospect of how I might be singled out or treated quickly disappeared during that first year in that special tool room. Primarily because we were all in the same boat, trying to learn this difficult skill trade. With so much to learn and such an opportunity to try and take advantage of, the atmosphere was more of us coming together to help one another, rather than pointing fingers at our differences. There were also two White women in our class.

Completing that first year and being assigned to a regular tool room impacted my thinking as to how I might be welcomed or not. My antennas were up, and it didn't take long for me to answer that question, it was actually the first night. The tool rooms that we were going to transition to got three weeks advanced notification that we were coming. They were told how many and who we were, I was one of three that went to the same tool room. We would later call ourselves the "Three Bs." The Beard, Jim Kistler, the Broad, Gloria Lang, and the

Black, me.

My first assignment was form grinding. This meant that I needed a journeyman to mentor me for several weeks. My first night in my new tool room, I was greeted by the foreman in charge of the afternoon shift. He showed me to my assigned work bench and gave me time to get settled in with my toolbox. Then it was time for me to meet my mentor/trainer; that's when the room started to stink. Keep in mind, the foreman had three weeks to find this person for me. Now here we go!

He comes to my work bench and asked me to follow him to the row of form grinders against the back wall; there is a journeyman working at each machine. I'm thinking that this is a simple meet and greet with my new mentor. However, that was not the case at all, this was a walk to find someone that would agree to train me. Not exactly a display of forward planning or class of any sort. I'm standing beside him, he introduces me to the first two journeyman and asked them if they would be willing to train me, they each said, "No." We found my mentor with the third try.

The foreman's station was in the middle of the tool room. We had to pass it to get to my work bench. When we got there, I stopped to let him know how I felt about what had just happened. I spoke at a volume level that was for his ears only. I began by reminding him that he had three weeks to sort this out, and that this entire embarrassing situation for me could have been avoided. I can't remember now if I ended calling him "an ignorant piece of shit" or "a classless piece of shit" but I do know that "piece of shit" was in there. He never apologized, but over time we developed a decent working relationship. First day in my new workplace was memorable for all the wrong reasons.

The lesson learned that caught me off guard and has stayed with me all these years also has to do with my interactions with a mentor form grinder. To complete your total hours on each machine, you have several rotations with the possibility of having different mentors. This was after my second rotation in form grinding with my second different mentor. I'll call him John to give him some identity.

The night in question began at my friend Jim Kistler's work bench. He was in the middle of his second rotation of form grinding with John as his mentor also. I noticed that he had a green grinding wheel sitting on his work bench. It stood out to me because I had never seen a green wheel before. I asked Jim where he got the wheel and what it was for. He explained that he had gotten it from John and that it was designed to help keep heat out of the metal when you are grinding.

When I mentioned earlier about my antennas being on high alert when I was assigned to my actual tool room, I was talking about signs of prejudice treatment toward me. After my first night, the environment always seemed pregnant with the possibility of showing me a new way to make me feel unwelcomed, the green wheel was the worse. You see, I always carried a mental notebook of how I was treated in Mississippi. I also knew that being the first Black in this capacity at this company in this tool room, was sure to add new chapters in my notebook. With that being said, the "green wheel" still caught me looking in a different direction.

This is why I was stunned. Being in this tool room for about two years, I thought that I had a pretty good handle on who I could trust, and who I couldn't; who liked me and who didn't; who wanted to see me succeed and who wanted me to fail, and who was just indifferent to my situation altogether. Truth is, I felt that there were a lot more people in my corner than not. John and I always had a good working relationship, and I felt that we were friends.

When I discovered that green wheel at Jim's bench, I had recently worked with John for several weeks on various jobs and he had never mentioned the benefits of a green wheel to me. My mental flashback didn't go to Mississippi but rather to something I heard when I was in high school. During the summer between my junior and senior years, I worked at a hand car wash that was owned by my stepfather's brother. The job wasn't particularly hard, and it didn't pay much money, but it was almost like a rite of passage for a young man facing adulthood head on. It was like going to school on life. The stories, the laughter, and the good times spent with the people who worked there and the ones just stopping by to kill time made it a unique summer job. The stories sometimes ran the limits of what your imagination could handle, two of them have stood out to me over the years.

One was told by a young man who was always being teased about his over-sized penis. He was talking one day about this girl he was dating, her sisters, and the condition of the house they were living in. He said that the house was so filthy that one day while he was there, the dog came in the house from being outside, took a dump, and went back outside. Because I can be a clean freak at times, his story was hard to wrap my brain around and hard to forget.

This second story was my flashback concerning the green wheel. My stepfather's brother told a story one day about an encounter he had on the streets of our city's downtown area with a White man. They had been arguing about something and the guy called him a Nigger. He said that he went back to his car, got a hatchet out of his trunk, ran the guy down, and started beating him with it. At some point, the man is down on the sidewalk bleeding profusely from several parts of his body, looks up and said, "And you're still a Nigger."

That story and that image caused me to picture my own story about John and the green wheel, and it goes something like this. Fred, you're a nice guy, you're probably going to get your journeyman's card, but "you're still a Nigger." You got invited to join the club, you got into the club house to look around, you'll probably be awarded a membership badge but, "you will never really get to be one of us!" That green wheel emotional memory was something I kept close to me from that point throughout my working career. It was a constant reminder to treat people like they treat you. Also, that not every smiling face or pat on the back that pretends to help you is in your corner for the good.

You can dislike a person or people while at the same time respect them for the very thing you dislike them for; let me explain. I disliked many of the White people I personally encountered and read about in the state of Mississippi during my technical training there in the Air Force. Years later, as I've lived most of my adult life up North, I came to respect those same people in Mississippi for not hiding or camouflaging their feelings. They didn't like Blacks, and they let you know that they didn't like you. Whereas I've encountered a lot of White people up North that didn't like me or Black people but pretended that they did.

Some Northerners were very clever and deceptive in hiding their true feelings, while some Southerners just put it in your face, "We don't like you." There is a reason I say that I can respect those people that tell you how they feel about you. This is it: When you know how people feel about you, you know how to deal with them.

My career's journey was sometimes difficult being Black and in the minority in most of the circles I had to function in. With that being said, I would be remiss and do a disservice if I didn't acknowledge all the White people that helped and supported me along my career path. If I started to list names, that list would be long and memorable for me. I will be forever grateful.

JACKIE ROBINSON & ME

Jackie Robinson was the first Black to play baseball in the Major Leagues. I was the first Black to go through Packard Electric's Tool and Die Apprentice program. Packard had been in existence for eighty-two years when I got in.

In 1943, Branch Rickey, team president and general manager of the Brooklyn Dodgers wanted to integrate the Dodgers. When Mr. Robinson was interviewed by Mr. Rickey to play for the Dodgers, he told him that he needed more than a good baseball player. He said that he needed someone strong enough to be able to take abuse, insults, and carry the flag for the Black race. After much thought and careful consideration, he accepted the challenge and took the job.

At some point, he felt like he really was carrying the race flag, and so did I. Being the first at anything can be pressure packed. He was carrying it for the nation. I was merely doing it for one company, in one city, in one state. Jackie Robinson was seen as the birth of a new spirit in terms of opening racial doors in sports in America, in the 1940s.

I feel that it would be presumptuous of me and unfair to take the comparison much further because he went through so much more than I had to deal with. However, with that being said, what I went through was no small matter to me. In preparation for this chapter, I read Mr. Robinson's book, "I never had it made; Jackie Robinson an autobiography." I wish that I had read it when I first got in the apprenticeship program. I would have been able to draw strength and encouragement from some of his struggles. I wanted to see if some of his bumps in the road mirrored some of mine.

This is part of my takeaway from reading his book. Of course, we both were exposed to racial prejudice, that comes as no surprise given the cultural divide in this country. Jackie got an opportunity because he was good at something; I got an opportunity and had to try and learn to be good at something. One of the biggest differences between Jackie and me is that he was a skilled baseball player. He grew up playing it, loved it, and became quite good at it. Being able to do his job as a baseball player was not something he ever had to question. I, on the other hand, did not grow up playing "tool and die" or dealing with any machinery more complicated than a lawn mower. Nothing I had previously done prepared me for the precise challenges of the tool and die skill trades world. I questioned my ability to do this for about the first two years of my apprenticeship.

The questioning and challenging myself was real. However, I had been preparing most of my life to do whatever was called for to not fail in the significant battles in my life; to never give up. Something I felt what we had in common was to push back against authority when we felt it necessary. There was an incident when Jackie stood his ground and had to deal with the legal system, there were two times in my career that called for legal intervention also. They weren't the same, but the basic principles were pushing back against injustice.

I also saw a documentary on Jackie Robinson. That piece and the book both highlighted that legal incident, it happened to him while he was in the Army. Mr. Robinson pushed back against authority when he was told to go to the back of the bus by the driver, when he thought that he was sitting next to a

White woman. This was on a bus on a military base in Texas; Jackie had read the Army regulation that had been recently sent out that stated, "No discrimination on any Army vehicle on any Army Post in the U.S.A." When Jackie refused to move, the driver called the military police, but he continued to resist.

They arrested him and charged him with insubordination. The military police were disrespectful and called him a Nigger. He still refused to back down. During his trial, he admitted that he told the arresting Private that, "If he ever called him a Nigger again, he would break him in two." Also at the trial, he was asked what the word Nigger meant. He said that his grandmother was a slave, and she told him that the definition of that word was a low, uncouth person. He then said that he didn't consider himself low or uncouth and not a Nigger at all. He was found "Not Guilty" on all charges. It was said that as a young man, he always railed against segregation and carried himself with a sense of dignity and a sense of purpose in a way that says, I will not be ignored; I will not be denied.

Perhaps I tried to compare some of my challenges to those of Mr. Robinson's because he also was the first to do something, but it was more than that. It was as much based on how much I admired and respected how he handled and stood up for himself. A gentleman in the Jackie Robinson documentary said, "The First is no good if there isn't a Second." The first can open a door and then the second creates a trend. That trend allows the door to stay open so that others can come through. I believe he was "spot on" with that.

LAWSUITS

We all at some points in our lives, have had the occasion to take a reflective look backward at some impactful end results to our lives, based on some tipping point/transitional decisions we've made. Some are difficult to recall, while others, we do with a certain sense of pride.

While preparing to write this chapter on "Money," I went to our filing cabinet and pulled a folder labeled "Legal." Contained within it were some documents from the past that I hadn't visited in years. Some were papers representing two incidents concerning my job. One dealt with me getting into the Tool and Die program and the other was challenging General Motors (G.M.) for equal pay when I was a salaried engineer.

The one with G.M., was a class action lawsuit that ended in a Consent Decree ruling against G.M. The action and decree were about how G.M. treated or mistreated the salaried Black employees; Huguley, ET AL V General Motors Corporation. It covered three states: Ohio, Michigan, and Indiana. It was filed July 15, 1983, and was finally settled October 15, 1991.

The adjustment period of the settlement was set up to last for five years. That time was to adjust and make up the pay disparity between the Black and White salaried employees. I didn't have a lot of personal involvement with the suit over that time period. Just the occasional meeting with Mr. Huguley and some financial support for our legal representation.

The "Charge of Discrimination," I filed against Packard Electric, was a different story, I was totally involved. I was charging discrimination for not being placed in one of their skill trades programs. On May 31, 1972, a letter was sent to the "Ohio Civil Rights Commission" that asked them to forward the charge to the Equal Employment Opportunity Commission (E.E.O.C.) and for both to investigate the charge. A follow-up letter with more details was sent, June 13, 1972.

The "Charge of Discrimination" is a form, Section #7 reads as follows; explain what unfair thing was done to you.

This is what I wrote:

"I signed up to be tested for Packard Electric's apprenticeship program. However, before being tested, I attended the free math course offered by Packard and completed it. I also received outside tutoring at the Joint Apprenticeship Program's office in Youngstown, Ohio. As a result of these

and other efforts, I was told that I received a high score on the actual test. In view of the fact that I scored high on the test but failed to accumulate enough overall points to place me in the apprenticeship program, I felt that I was discriminated against in the remaining categories."

The accumulation of points for the program is the test score, being in the military and several categories based on their discretion like, high school grades, experience, and maybe, but not spoken, the color of your skin. The test score yielded the most points by far, which I scored high on. Plus, my high school grades were good, and I was in the military. Getting in should not have been a problem.

This charge was actually charged after the second time I tested/tried to get in the program. The first time was an experience that left me very frustrated. Several Blacks also tested that first time and none of us got into the program. I was one of the last to be called in to get the results of getting in the program or not. All the ones that had gone in before me, told me what to expect.

Each person was given the same reason as to why they didn't get in. They were told that they did good with everything on the test except math. Then they were encouraged to take the math class that they were offering and come back and test again. That was the class I mentioned in my discrimination charge.

When they told me that, I smiled because the math on the test didn't get harder than 9th grade algebra. I said to myself that there is no way in hell, they could use that to keep me out because I took all the advanced math courses at my school, algebra, advanced algebra, geometry, and trigonometry.

I was wrong. I got the very same speech; did good in everything except math. I asked if he had seen my high school transcripts. He opened my file, looked at it, paused, and said that maybe I got overconfident. My response was, "Overconfident, I don't think so, I want to see my test results!" He said that he couldn't because it was against the rules. What he said next and how he said it is something I have never forgotten.

He said that I should take the math course that they were offering, and with a full exaggerated smile said, "You do that, and you'll be right back in the old ball game." That was punctuated with a fist pump! I took the course, tested for the program again and was successful on that second try. I filed the discrimination charge before getting the results of the second test; I was anticipating some more game playing. I later had to drop it because I did get in the program.

I fought to get in that program because my approach to work has always been this, "I have enough friends, I go to work to make money." Skilled trades is where the hourly money is; Tool and Die is the highest paying skilled trade. It's only now, years later, that I have the vantage point of realizing the end result of that fight. That being, I got in the tool and die apprenticeship program. Back then, I knew that this was an important fight, but I couldn't fully grasp the long-term value it would have on shaping my career. Taking that action back then reflects a side of me that I don't ever want to forget; fighting for something that has worth and value.

SIDE HUSTLES

That first year in the Apprentice Tool Room was spent on the day-turn shift. Even though I got a raise in pay coming into the program, I was actually making less money. That's because my previous job came with "over time." There was no "over time" in the tool room that first year. Less take home pay meant that adjustments/sacrifices would have to be made on the home front. My wife and I understood that this would be short term, and we made the necessary adjustments. Understanding the end result benefits didn't lessen the financial impact on our young family as time marched on.

About four months into the program, I had an opportunity to pick up a part-time job working with a friend of mine, Tyrone

(Ty). He also had a full-time job and was doing home remodeling on the side. He saw that I had some skills in that area and invited me to join him because he was working alone. Ty had several jobs lined up and we were a good team. The extra income felt good and welcomed until one fateful night that caused me to question everything about this side hustle.

Ty and I had priced out a full kitchen remodel job for a co-worker of his, Gary, who lived in an area called Lake Milton. It was a typical small community that was built up and identified by this lake. While Gary was waiting on financial approval for his job, a neighbor of his inquired as to who was going to be doing his work. This neighbor had built a new house behind his current house and was putting on the finishing touches before moving in. This was his dream house that he and his wife had been saving years for. He asked Gary, to ask Ty, if he would come out and quote some of the remaining work.

Ty went out and quoted the work, it wasn't a lot; finish the shower in the bathroom and do the backsplash in the kitchen. They agreed on the price. Ty and I thought that it would serve as a nice filler until Gary's financing was approved. We would be installing a popular product back then called Marlite. It was fairly easy to work with and came in 4X8 sheet paneling and needed to be glued on with a paste.

Having full-time day jobs, it's always late when we get to a job site. It's day two, we made all the cuts and started installing in the bathroom shower. That went well, and we proceeded to the kitchen. We had finished putting the paste/glue on the backsplash areas. We went to get the first piece to install when we heard and saw a heart pounding event that seemed impossible. It was a wall of flames. It looked to me like the whole world was on fire. The homeowners were preparing to move in and had the gas turned on that day. We knew that the gas was not on the day before and didn't notice that the gas pilot light on the stove was now on. The paste that we were using was highly flammable. The sound we heard was like one you would hear when lighting something fueled by propane only ten times louder.

The entire backsplash was on fire, all the way from the stove to the refrigerator. It's about 2:00 a.m. This was before cell phones, and they didn't have phone service turned on yet; we had no ability to call for help. We grabbed towels and rags and was able to beat the fire out. That was the most scared I had ever been in my life. Thankfully, the fire is out, and we are assessing the damage. It wasn't as bad as first seemed, only the hood over the stove and the under sides of the cabinets were damaged, no harm to the stove, refrigerator, or the counter tops. We clean up as best as we could and now it's about 3:30

a.m. We know that the husband is home alone in the front house because his wife worked the midnight shift and stopped by to pay us on her way to work.

It's very dark as Ty and I are knocking on the back door to deliver the bad news. After several knocks two separate times, there was no response from inside the house. Suddenly, a cat came screaming from behind a tree. In pitch darkness, a loud cat, acting like it was looking for a fight, was the final exclamation point on top of what was already a very scary night. We decided not to knock a third time. We left there almost running.

The next day, Ty didn't go to work. Gary got the news as to what happened at his neighbor's house from his neighbor. Gary called Ty. Ty went through the sequence of events and that we tried to inform his neighbor, but he didn't come to the door. What Gary said next was also scary. Gary had a second job as a deputy sheriff for Lake Milton. He explained that a few weeks before this fire, his neighbor was in a bar fight in one of the local pubs. He said that it took three deputies to restrain him. He was a big guy, and it sounded like he was tough too. Gary then said that if he had opened the door and received the news that we had set his new house on fire, it would have been a lot of physical bad news for us.

We paid for all of the repairs and that was the end of our

working relationship; I quit. I looked at what I was doing and what I was earning and compared it to what I was risking and giving up. I looked at our previous jobs, calculated the hours against the pay and discovered that I was making less per hour than I was on my day job. I also balanced everything against time spent away from home.

Whenever I go through something notable in my life, I try and look for lessons learned. That part-time hustle fire was certainly noteworthy, it made me understand that there can be down sides to anything, no matter how good it might first appear. It taught me to take a deep dive into anything I might consider doing going forward, anything and everything.

If Ty and I hadn't reacted the way that we did, that entire house could have burnt down in the middle of that night. We would have been responsible and liable. We weren't licensed for some of the things we were doing. We weren't bonded to cover ourselves in case something went wrong. We were just two hard working guys hustling on the side to make a few extra bucks. One lesson learned for me was that hard work doesn't always equate to smart work. Sometimes when you take short cuts, you can get cut short. We were lucky, fortunate, blessed, pick one. We were looking to get paid that night and instead it could have been a total financial disaster. One of the things I say to myself now before taking something on is this, "Before you accept the work, do your homework; count the cost!"

Another side-hustle venture I got involved with wound up with me being equal partners in a tool grinding business. I had my journeyman's card at this time. It started off with me and three other journeymen tool and die makers wanting to start a small tool and die or machine shop. We met with the Small Business Administration (S.B.A.), seeking a start-up loan. Ultimately, that meeting became the source of another lesson learned for me.

At the meeting, their representative asked us a question, "Which one of you are going to quit your job and head this up?" Each of us started looking around the room like we didn't understand the question. After a few moments of total silence, he went on to say, "If none of you believe in it enough to quit your job, why should we?" We left there disappointed but quickly came up with a plan. We decided to buy this tool grinding company in Warren, Ohio, Quality Tool Grinding Service. The plan was to grow the business then go back to the S.B.A., show them what we were capable of and ask for another loan. We did grow the business, but the long story is complicated, the short story is that it didn't work out. However, my takeaway lesson learned was a reminder of one of life's byproducts. If you don't believe in what you are doing, it will surface, and it will be problematic.

FINAL MONEY-TRAIN STOP

Money drives emotions and changes. It can be a very powerful change agent, one of the most impactful changes it can promote is independence. Not all, but some of our money decisions have to be carefully balanced against risk and reward. When you're in the game, you have to know the rules. Money comes with a lot of rules that are tied to laws.

When I was in my childhood, preteen years, I wasn't focused on things like being rich or poor, but I felt like we as a family were doing OK. My father and his brother, Uncle Bill, had a plastering business. It had all the appearances and trappings of a successful business. They got new cars every two years; my father liked Chryslers and Uncle Bill preferred Buicks, although he did have a 1956 Thunderbird. They also had a Cabin Cruiser boat for summer fun at the lakes plus the trucks, equipment, and crew personnel needed to run the business.

They were riding pretty high for a small-town venture. They tried their hands at a variety of investments that didn't pan out, but they tried. Two I can remember are starting a Pork and Bean business and investing in an oil well drilling company. That oil drilling struck a bed of water, not oil. They even sponsored a Miss Bronze America beauty contest. A nice picture of "Money your friend," then something happened, the IRS, Internal Revenue Service.

My father and uncle were the hardest working people on their crew. However, they weren't the crew, they owned the business and didn't know all the rules of the business game. They didn't know some of the legal aspects; how to properly keep the books and meet the government standards for the financial rules and laws. They weren't trying to skirt the law, there were just some things they didn't know. Seemingly overnight, their world, our world was turned upside down. The business was gone. Not because of the IRS but rather the housing trends were turning more towards "dry walling" and away from "plastered walls." Another huge factor was the health of Uncle Bill. He started developing migraine headaches from the plastering dust.

My parents divorced. We moved in with our grandparents across the street. My father moved to New Jersey to work for a family friend. Uncle Bill started driving big rig trucks and was killed in a trucking accident. That "Money your friend," has the ability to turn into your "Devastating Foe" and change your world with no mercy. It felt like all of this happened within a heartbeat to our families.

It's important that each of us figures out our definition of success, the sooner, the better. For some, it begins and ends with money and wealth; pursuing that in and of itself, is nothing wrong. But, how you go after it and the price you pay along the way can be devastating. When it comes to money, societal norms and pressures can impact every fiber of your being, if you let it; I suggest that you don't. Some things that money should not control is who you are at your core, that means your personality and what your moral compass reflects.

There's a popular phrase, "do you," that I believe holds great value. It simply means "be yourself." Being yourself, while also considering the bigger picture, might call for necessary compromise occasionally, calculating the cost. However, staying true to you affords you the best opportunity to be comfortable with yourself. In the end you'll be happier for it whether it cuts against the societal grains or not!

CHAPTER 8

-LEADERSHIP

"Future Leader," should be stamped on every birth certificate.

There have been many books written on leadership and leaders: good leaders, bad leaders, leaders of Industry, political leaders, leaders of science and of social conscience, just to name a few. Also books on a variety of leadership styles, we can learn from many if not all of those publications. While many of those books are backed up with years of study and data that details their end result opinions, my chapter on "Leadership" isn't that deep or detailed. I'm simply going to speak on what I believe are some basic truths.

Admittedly, I will probably not be someone that will ever be compared to many of the famous authors on the subject. However, I'm still hopeful that sharing my lifetime of sometimes leading groups and observing others in leadership positions will be helpful to some of you. What I'm going to share are components of and things that apply to most forms of leadership.

There are many things in life that are outside of our control: things like the sun rising and setting, the number of hours in a day, the weather, and countless number of situational things that we constantly have to react to. The things we can't control far out-number those that we can. However, there is one that we do control, it has the ability to help us in all situations and can actually give us the advantage in many cases. That's the control we have over ourselves and how we react to things we face.

I noted in the chapter "**Transition**," that life is made up of about 20% of things that actually happens to us and 80% of how we react to them. I believe that a large portion of the 80% has to do with how we see ourselves as leaders and the level of leadership skills we have acquired. Understanding that makes it easier to acknowledge the various different outcomes to the same situation or set of circumstances. Leadership is only one thing that gets factored in, there can be many others. While that is true, I believe that it's one of the biggest parts of the final decision in most cases.

Leadership: A simple definition is that leadership is the

act of motivating a group of people to act toward achieving a common goal. He or she is the person in the group that possesses the combination of personality and leadership skills that makes others want to follow his or her directions.

Leader: (*noun*) The person who leads or commands a group, organization, or country.

I think that the accepted definition of "leader" is a bit short sighted. It does not identify a portion of society that a person also leads or commands, us. We are the "leaders" of ourselves.

This is my definition of Leader: (*noun*) The person who leads or commands Themselves, a group, organization, or country.

Throughout our lives it seems like a battle is constantly being waged over the question, "Are you a leader or a follower?" I have also heard the basic premise of that question phrased, "Are you a thermostat or a thermometer?" The follower is led by the leader and the thermometer is controlled by the thermostat. If you have never done anything that fits the society definition of a leader, then it suggests that you have been a follower your entire life, or have you?

When most people think about leadership, they tend to think about leaders or "The Leader." Their minds drift toward the direction that only leaders are responsible for leadership. However, if you buy into my position that each one of us is the leader of ourselves, then each of us are capable of leadership activities. Leadership is something none of us can escape. Whether we seek it or shy away from it does not matter, that only determines the level we might be willing to participate at.

That means that it matters not whether a person is heading up the group/ organization, or just a member, they can exhibit leadership skills. This is also true of us as individuals when we are not partaking in something organized. When you start to understand the concept that you are the leader of yourself, you begin to understand that you can represent some type of leadership. To that end, you also start to recognize that not all leadership is good. To personalize that, "We don't always represent the best parts of ourselves. We don't always act the best that we should." It's not that we can't, it's more because at times we choose not to. It's always a choice and sometimes we make bad decisions.

We don't always think about leadership when we are in crowded places. However, we've all seen people act in various ways in those scenarios and have come away with opinions on those actors. While your first reaction might be that the person or persons are acting in a range from very bad to very good, subconsciously you might be saying that you either would or wouldn't want this person or people on your team.

Regardless as to who you are, most people that take time to get involved with something want that something to be worthy of their time and effort. They want it to turn out favorably to the end target of the project or cause. In other words, few people join something looking forward to failure. People don't want bad actors or people displaying questionable leadership on their team.

Understanding the relationship between "Leadership" and "Leader" can be very useful as we aspire to different things or positions in life. Most leaders got to those positions by showing and developing good leadership skills over time.

This touches a little on something I talk about in the chapter **"How Do You Know Who You Know."** In this chapter, I talk about something I call a life formula, $P/T=R$; Perception over Time equals Reality. If a person over a period of time shows leadership abilities, people can start to see them as a leader; one builds on the other.

There has always been the debate as to whether leaders and heroes are born or shaped over time. I choose not to join that conversation. What I will say is that from personal experience and observation, leadership is a process of trial and error. Those who pay the most attention and learn from that process seem to reap the better fruits that life has to offer at every level. That statement does not just speak to status or material things, in fact, some of our more meaningful things in life have to do with our personal relationships. For me, it seems like the older I get, the more I see the proof of that.

I believe the question, "Are you a leader or a follower?" is a bit flawed, I view it as somewhat of a trick question. Leader and follower can and often are synonyms with each other.

Leaders or the heads of something need to show leadership skills. Also, anyone that is a member/follower of something, not the head, with the understanding that they have the power to lead themselves, can also display their leadership skills. Leaders and followers are both capable of showing some type of leadership; skilled or perhaps not so much.

When you look in the mirror, what or who do you see? Besides the obvious physical reflection, who is the real person actually looking back at you? Is it a strong confident you that is ready to take on the world; a you that has been broken by life's circumstances; a you that you no longer recognize or perhaps a you that is still trying to figure out who you are and what you want out of life? Or, how about this, do you see yourself as a leader? If you don't, then you need to start because you are!

How you actually look is important for sure, but in the grand scheme of living life, how you feel about yourself is far more important. We have all seen beautiful people, by most standards with low self-esteem, making a hot mess of their lives. Beauty is always fleeting to some degree.

When I was in high school, I played football all four years. We were a dynasty. However, it was not one you would ever brag about. We never won a game for the whole four years. That's right, a losing dynasty. Sometimes when I think about it, I laughingly wonder how I'm able to get out of bed so easily. One would think that being part of something that notably bad would leave mental scars to last a lifetime. Truth is, it didn't, and I sometimes wonder why. I don't think we thought much about it after we turned our uniforms in at the end of each season.

During the process of writing this book, I thought about a lot of things that I've either done or was a part of. The topic of playing football and never tasting victory kept speaking to me. It was like a life lesson that I needed to address but I didn't know what to make of I, that is until I started thinking about this chapter on "leadership."

For the first time, I quit letting it be this random thought that would pop up sometimes, mostly during football season, and decided to do a deep dive into how I really felt. Putting this down on paper gave me a feeling somewhere between embarrassment and something way less than a sense of pride. I never had these feelings in high school and now I'm wondering why. Why didn't we label ourselves as losers back then? This is my assessment of my feelings now versus back in high school. Now, it's part of history and I have to look at it for what it is. Four years with never winning a single game, how does that even happen!

I think that back in high school, most of us didn't see ourselves as just football players, but rather as athletes, and good athletes. Most of us also played other sports with varying degrees of success. There were people on our team that played basketball and ran track. These were two sports that our school was known to field very good teams. I held the high and low hurdle records at the school for several years, just saying.

At the end of each season, we knew that we played on a team that didn't win a game, again! At season's end however, there was no one saying that they had enough and wouldn't be back for the next year. It was more like a feeling of we'll get'em next year. Maybe we were treating it like the Cleveland Browns chasing a Super Bowl Championship, maybe next year, who knows.

Here's what I do know, I enjoyed playing football. I liked playing with my teammates, it was fun. I really liked game day and the physical contact; I LOVED hitting people. When I think back on those years, I realize the value in how a person sees himself. We never saw ourselves as losers.

How you see and analyze yourself is very important, it can help or hurt you in making plans to move forward. It can help or hurt you to strive for the future that you want to see for yourself. Knowing where you are and where you want to go is vital to one's mental state of mind. When a person is unsure of his or her current and future directions or goals, it tends to promote an atmosphere of instability.

Back to the question, "Are you a leader or a follower?"

When parents are raising their children, that's a question they have either verbalized or have had it bounced around in their minds. Caring, responsible parents have always been concerned about the company their kids surround themselves with. This is mostly true because of that question. You see, it takes time and some influence before children start to develop a sense of who they are. This is why parents are not sure if they are raising someone that is a leader, when the kids gather to do things, or someone who will just go along with the crowd. I think that this is why the word "follower" is associated sometimes with negative connotations. It evokes thoughts of people blindly following someone or something while giving up their own sense of reasoning and thoughts.

When I think about that question and how it relates to adults, I see the only difference being the responsibilities assigned to each word. I don't see them as one being good, the "leader" and the other, "follower" being bad or something to avoid. I say that because I view it through the lens of leadership. When you believe that you are the leader of yourself, you can easily belong to or be a member/follower of any group or organization and not let it do your thinking. As a member you can showcase your leadership skills and be a productive part of all the activities of the group without surrendering the most vital parts of you; what your core values are and to be able to express yourself during the discussions of issues.

I actually think that these two persons, leader and follower, are more closely linked than what they might seem at first glance. When a leader of a group steps down and either remains within that group or joins another as something other than the leader, they probably become good members/followers. I believe this to be true because as a leader, they personally know and appreciate the efforts of hard working members that were on their team and the helpful difference they may have made. This serves as a constant reminder as to ways they can benefit the leader of the group they find themselves in.

I have had the privilege of leading several different types of groups. Some in the corporate sector and some in smaller settings at different churches I was a member of. In the smaller arenas like church and social organizations, I have become a strong advocate of keeping the leaders in place for only a few years at a time. The reason being, I believe that it makes for a stronger group/organization over time. I feel that way for the reason I mentioned earlier; past leaders becoming strong members.

To that end, I've held the view that the strength of a group can be measured two different ways, either by the strength of its leader, or by the strength of the weakest link within the group. There can be arguments made supporting both.

If you have strong leadership at the top, the leader, and he or she is effective and has the right motives, the group can be strong and advance the overall agendas in positive ways. However, we all know plenty of examples of strong leaders with wrong or questionable intentions. One of the worst examples is Adolf Hitler as the German leader.

I think that the better group/organization is one filled with members with experience and good leadership skills. I believe that this is the type of organization our forefathers had in mind when they considered how the United States should best be governed, a three-part balance of power. That's what I call the strength of the weakest link.

Life comes at us fast and carries with it the possibility of change. This is another area where leadership can have some impact. When our circumstances change, we have to and need to debate our response.

I had someone tell me once, "Any plan that can't be changed is not a good one." Over time, I found that to be a true statement for planning life in general. It's especially true when the plans are being formulated within a group or organization. If at the end of the planning session everyone is in agreement that this direction is the ONLY road to success, you need to start over. That plan is not a good one. I say that because often times, things show up once projects are started that weren't foreseen during the planning phase. If there aren't plans in place to adjust for change, plans B, C, and or D, your project could be seriously jeopardized.

Sometimes when life changes and we find ourselves caught up in it, we hesitate with our direction forward for what could be a variety of reasons. I believe that one of the more common reasons is because we don't have a proper vision of ourselves. We don't see ourselves as leaders.

One of the jobs of a leader, besides being successful at the task they are responsible for, is to build leadership skills within the group and promote teamwork. At one point in my life, I was the Chairman of the Trustee Board at my church. That Board was responsible for the physical up-keep and maintenance of the buildings and the grounds. Also, any legal matters pertaining to the church.

When we purchased our church, it was a large brick three

story school that sat on four acres. The obvious challenge was to convert it into a building that would meet the needs of the church. We used most of the classrooms as classrooms and converted the cafeteria and gym into our sanctuary. Some years later, we built a new sanctuary and attached it to the old one, the original school. So, as you can see, there was a lot of property the Trustees were responsible for. Incidentally, the school was the elementary school I attended growing up, how cool is that.

After several years at the helm of this board, I woke up one day with what I thought was a brilliant idea. You see, the school was old and in constant need of many things. It was difficult to identify and stay on top of all the problems that needed our limited resources. My idea was to break the church into sections or departments and assign two- person teams to oversee each area, such as: electrical, plumbing, outside grounds, carpentry, painting, etc. The plan was that each team would be responsible for maintaining their area and if something big surfaced they would bring it to the attention of the entire board at a monthly meeting. At that point, it would be put on the works agenda to be prioritized and resources assigned for the fix. Emergencies would not have to wait until the next monthly meeting. Nothing would no longer fall through the cracks, brilliant right? WRONG!

This was a total failure and had to soon be abandoned. You see, most of the two-person teams were made up of people that were used to being told what to do. They were not used to leading, telling others what to do. Neither felt empowered to lead the other. Perhaps because they didn't see themselves as leaders. This is one of several examples why I believe that the true strength of most small groups is the strength or make-up of its weakest links.

I learned from that experience. We went back to handling things with the entire Trustee Board, but with a twist; I had one more trick up my sleeve. When we came up with a project, it was assigned to a "Champion" with the intentions of making sure that person was not the Chairman of the Board. It seemed like there was something magical about making someone a Champion. There seemed to be something empowering about the word Champion. They started to see themselves a little differently, they started to see themselves as leaders. I'm happy to report that this approach had much better results. We were strengthening our Board by building leaders within our ranks.

One indicator of good leadership is how the group performs in the absence of its leader. When a group has good leadership, very few people outside of the group know when the leader is absent. The reason the contacts or customers are not aware is because the group is still totally functional. They continue doing everything that needs to be done without a drop-off in performance.

A poorly led team has much the opposite results. The team/ group falls apart when the leader is absent and functions poorly. This could be for many reasons. The problem could be that the leader is strong and likes to be in total control but has not properly learned the values of allocating responsibilities or delegating within the group. Sometimes, it could be because a leader feels that no one knows as much as he or she does about running the operation and that makes them the most valuable; the M.V.P. of the group. Another possible problem within a poorly functioning group is the lack of training. The leader might know how everything works and should function but might not want to take the time or perhaps doesn't have the temperament to pass that knowledge throughout the group to train them.

I believe that there are certain things a good leader needs to strive for to allow or help the group/organization to function at a high level. A leader needs to have a good understanding of how the group fits within the larger organization and what those expectations are. Also, they need to know the politics of the organization, what rules are hard and fast, and which ones can be fudged a little. A leader should learn the strengths and weaknesses of the group, mostly the personnel make-up.

A leader needs to figure out a way to make each member of the team feel important and a valued part of everything that happens. They need to understand how the group is viewed within the total organization; excellent, average, or poor performing.

The leader is responsible for promoting a healthy workplace. Maintaining an environment where everyone's human rights are respected and protected. They need to take the temperature of the atmosphere, that simply means observing the attitude of the personnel. Are they mostly frowning and complaining, or can you have a little fun from time to time? Is there a lot of tension or is it somewhat light and airy? It's never the same all the time for different reasons, but a leader needs to keep striving for a workspace that people enjoy and can execute their duties at the highest levels possible.

The leader needs to be predictable, that means to be the same every day as much as possible. If you're a good guy, be a good guy, if you're an asshole then be an ass all the time. It causes instability when the team doesn't know what they are facing from day to day, not knowing promotes a lot of tension. A leader needs to be rock-steady to whatever their personality is. Speaking of personalities, anyone fortunate enough to get promoted to a leadership position should make sure that only their title and responsibility changes, not their personality.

A leader has to sometimes be a cheerleader and find ways to keep the team motivated and upbeat. It's been said that "People won't care how much you know until they know how much you care." I found that to be a true statement because most things in life, involving people, comes back to personal relationships.

Leaders have to understand that flexibility is part of good leadership because circumstances and conditions often change, when they do, changes might be necessary to maintain order; sometimes, that means knowing when to transmit and when to receive. It's been said, "You're not learning when you're talking." Leaders can't be afraid of change; they also need to admit when they are wrong or have made mistakes and not blame others or make a lot of excuses.

Good leaders learn when to fight and when to walk away, that generally comes with experience over time. They learn to choose wisely; not every battle is worth fighting. Sometimes as a leader you are tasked with making hard decision. As the leader of oneself, there is something that I've learned over time that holds great value and we control it. I call it "The integrity of the tongue." When it comes to communications, there are certain things we all should avoid and know; lying is problematic while "saying what you mean and meaning what you say" are foundational to good leadership.

I found one more that should be added to that list, and it hardly gets mentioned. It's been phrased, "When you find a dog that will bring a bone, that same dog will take one." Simply put, that's a person that was told something in private, promised to keep it there but has no problem with violating that trust and passing the information forward. The person receiving the information might find it useful but will ultimately see that person as being someone not to trust. Don't be that person. Always keep your entrusted bones to yourself; keep your integrity tongue trustworthy.

There were some very tough decisions I've had to make concerning two churches, me and my family were members of. At both churches, I held some leadership positions within various groups. Those positions came with responsibilities that I took seriously. I always tried to do my best to make a positive difference and uphold the standards of whatever group/organization I found myself part of. My decisions were to leave both churches.

The first was a church that was basically founded by two families. My first wife's family was one of the two. The congregation was small which presented the normal problems that comes with not having the members and or finances to address things you want to do and sometimes need to do. There was a period we were without a permanent Senior Pastor. I was on the committee to search for one to lead our congregation. That search led us to interview a young man that had recently graduated from seminary school. He was highly recommended from that school and interviewed very well. This would be his first opportunity to lead a church.

I represented our committee and addressed the congregation with the recommendation for him as our possible new Pastor, this came with a date for his trial sermon. Things went well, and I was chosen again to get in front of the church to recommend that we vote to make him our next permanent Pastor, and we did.

As time went on, I started to notice some things in his private life that was disturbing to me. I confronted him about it, and he denied what I had accused him of. I didn't reveal my source to him, but I knew he was not being truthful.

After much prayer between me and my wife, we made the hard decision to leave the church. When we did, we never told anyone our real reason for leaving. We simply stated that it was time for us to move on. We didn't want to be a disruption or cause confusion within the congregation. We felt that if what we were leaving for was true, they would eventually see it for themselves.

After leaving that church, we joined a church that presented an even harder decision to leave. My first wife died while we were members there and my total tenure was twenty-nine years. This was a church that I truly loved.

Several years after we joined, the Senior Pastor left for a high-level position with the head of our denomination: The Southern Baptist Convention. When my new wife and I finally left, the leadership Senior Pastor had changed hands several times. The reason for leaving this church was because we, well mostly me, didn't like the direction the overall church leadership was heading.

I have always felt that you have a better chance at fixing a problem being someone on the inside as opposed to being on the outside. However, inside fighting comes with its own unique set of problems, in most cases, a lot of disruption. For me, again after much prayer, the better decision was to leave rather than to stay and fight against the new direction of the current leadership.

With both departures, the heart of my decisions to leave was this; I saw myself as a leader at both churches and I believe that many in both congregations did also. I strongly feel that as a leader, when you stay within a small voluntary organization and follow that leadership, you are being seen as putting your stamp of approval on it. When other people see that, and they respect you, they think all is well. With me feeling that all was not well, I felt to a certain degree that I was misleading people that looked up to me. I also felt that to make the strongest statement as to what and how I was really feeling about things, was to make the hard decision to just leave and move on to someplace that better represented my values.

I mentioned that I have experienced leadership roles within small groups like my church and also within a large corporation. While there are some similarities from a leadership perspective, there are also a lot of differences. There was a great deal more that I had to learn and adjust to in the corporate world, I found some of those lessons to be emotionally painful but necessary.

Some years before I became a Supervisor in Engineering, I worked in the tool room system as a Tool and Die Journeyman. That was a world of tight precision and there was only one story to tell. Either the piece you were working on was within tolerance or it was scrap, that was it, only one story to tell. That story was about what I did, for the most part I was representing myself.

To go from the tool room representing me, to one day being a Supervisor of one of several groups within a Superintendent's area was like the difference between night and day. I was going from hard facts representing one story into a very competitive environment where there are stories within stories. However, this was like most things in life, when you find yourself in the middle of change, the faster you learn the better off you become.

While I was developing my style of leadership for my group, I was always watching how some of the other supervisors were handling their business; particularly this one guy. I noticed one day that all of his people had new phones. On another occasion, everybody had new computers on their desks. With all of us under the same Superintendent, his group was starting to stand out. The rest of us at that time, had nothing new.

I wanted to know how he was making this happen, so I scheduled a meeting with him. What he shared was very enlightening. He helped me to look at my job from a different angle which caused me to change my approach to certain things. One of the things that I learned was the importance of being able to present your position on your agenda items, how you tell your story.

He reminded me that every Supervisor had things that they wanted to do within their groups. He said that it's not always the best ideas that gets funded and moves forward, it's sometimes the best stories about the ideas. What he said next was a game changer for me. He explained that when you are in an area like we were in, many groups under the same Superintendent, he determines how his limited resources (his budget) is dispersed between the groups. He said that part of my success for providing for my group would depend on how well I could sell my story.

He left me with this, "Whatever you are trying to push forward, give it a lot of thought, choose your words carefully, and focus on your salesmanship skills. Good leaders are good salesmen." This was a big help because it was early in my new position, and I really appreciated it.

There was another piece of advice that served me well when I first went from the hourly ranks into salary, from the tool room into engineering. I was not a Supervisor at this time, this came from another tool maker that had also moved to engineering. After about a week in the department, he told me this, "Don't let your boss be surprised with something you've done. Make sure that any bad or potentially bad news is delivered to him or her by you, not someone else. Also, when you share that news, have a plan or some suggestions as to how to rectify or neutralize the problem." That conversation was unexpected but very welcomed, I say unexpected because I remembered how I was first treated in my early days going into the tool room; It was anything but welcoming.

One of the things I had to change about my supervising style was my approach to how I interacted with my boss, the

Superintendent. I felt that one of my core responsibilities was to keep his phone from ringing by my customers about problems concerning my group. I didn't want to involve him with helping to solve our problems. I felt strongly that it was my job to address and fix any situation confronting us. I felt good about that approach because he was getting plenty of customer calls concerning some of the other groups that he had to get involved with. I felt that style was working for me until something changed within his area, that change was a new direction for how raises (money) were going to be handled.

There would be an all-day conference where each Supervisor would have up to five minutes to present each person in their group. The presentations were to point out what they were responsible for, also anything you wanted to point out about their involvements over the past twelve months. What was added and different was that each Supervisor would vote on how they felt on that person's contribution to their group and by extension, the organization.

I felt that this system was seriously flawed for a variety of reasons. However, this was the new game in town. The voting was done by the numbers 1-5, with 5 being the best. The Superintendent would leave with all the calculations, and he would have the final say. This change drove me to change how I dealt with the boss going forward, here's why. As some of the Supervisors were presenting their people, I started to take note on the comments the boss was making on some of these individuals. Comments like, I remember that, oh yea, they did a good job on getting us out of that jam, or that was a critical fix, it made a big difference. The thing that I really noticed was that most of his remarks were about the engineers that were in groups that seemed to be always needing his help. These were the groups that kept his phone ringing.

The conference the following year was much different in how the boss viewed my group. That was due mostly to the change that I made. I started having conversations with him about the problem-solving efforts that went on in my group. I would detail the situation and point out the different scenarios if things were not handled properly. I would also praise the hard work of the people involved; this was information in real time. This painted a picture as to what could have happened but didn't, what could have spoiled his day but didn't. He remembered a lot of what I shared at that next conference, mission accomplished, and there was a noticeable difference in the monies received for my group that year.

Sometimes, when change is necessary to address an issue, the first thing that's tried might not work. When your attitude is right, your misses should not discourage you from continuing to try. Each miss should be viewed as a learning experience. Truth is that most first-time fixes don't completely re-solve all the problems. Truth is, it's times like these that tend to shine a light on one's leadership skills.

When I was in the tool room, one of my Supervisors had a somewhat unique leadership style. In fact, most things about him were unique. He was smart, brash, cocky, and whether true or not, presented an air about himself that said, "I don't really care what you think about me." He also had a personal-ity that was unique. We've all heard people described as "you either love them or hate them, there's no in between." Feel-ings for this guy would range from different levels of "like" to "hate," I don't think anybody was feeling the "love." He was able to evoke those types of emotions from the people in the workplace.

One day, I saw him take a tool maker into the office and give him a "contact," that's disciplinary action on him. They left the office laughing and the tool maker bought the Supervisor a cup of coffee. That was somewhat confusing to me, so when I got the chance I asked the Supervisor about it. His response to my question was a good life lesson for me and was really helpful when I became a Supervisor a few years later.

My question was, "How do you give someone a contact, and they buy you coffee?"

He said, "I didn't give him a contact, he gave himself a contact." He explained that he had warned this guy that the next time he comes in late, the contact was going to happen. He went on to say he came in late, so I simply did what I said I was going to do.

I asked him if he understood why he was getting the contact. He said "Yes," then I said, "Come on, buy me a cup of coffee." Like I said, he was different.

His lesson for me was this, he said, "Fred, don't make threats you don't back up. If you do, your words become like a paper tiger, non-threatening and useless. Understand that your words will count for something in situations like that. They will either represent your strength or your weakness." I think that is good advice for anyone that is in or seeking a leadership position, it was good for me.

"A mind is a terrible thing to waste." June 15, 2013, we were introduced to this iconic slogan. It was meant to promote the United Negro College Fund scholarship program for Black students. The first time I heard that advertised on television, I had a flash back to a time in my youth. I'm thinking it was somewhere between my sophomore and junior years in high school, during the sixties. The story associated with this flash back would probably be better suited and placed within a chapter titled "Foolishness." However, I'm not planning on writing that chapter, although I probably could, given my lifetime of some misadventures. I decided to tell this story here because it fits the narrative of self-leadership.

This was not a misadventure as much as it was a mindset way of thinking. This was also during the time frame that my mother had remarried, and we were living with my stepfather. He was in the sanitation business, a "garbage man." It doesn't sound very glamorous, but it was a good job. It gave him access and opportunities to cross paths with a lot of interesting people. Some of those people were very colorful and sketchy to say the least.

One summer day, a Cadillac pulls up in the driveway. My stepfather summons my mother and me (we were the only one's home at the time) to join him in greeting whoever was in this car. A man jumped out wearing very flashy clothes and adorned with a lot of eye popping jewelry; "Home Boy" was clean as a Motel mop. He directed us to the back of the car and opened the trunk. The trunk was full of brand new clothes. As he was shuffling through them and pointing out the different sizes, I felt like I was standing in front of a salesman at some department store. I was trying to wrap my head around what was seemingly being presented as a normal day and way of shopping.

I actually thought that this was pretty cool; private, specialized shopping. You just needed to walk out your front door, with some cash in your pocket; this was not credit card or writing a check kind of shopping, that was clear. Not only did we buy a few pieces, we put in an order for styles and sizes for his next visit. While he was the only one that initially got out of the car, there were three young women accompanying him that stayed seated. After a few minutes of shopping, they also exited the car. At that point, everything changed for me. I went from shopping to gawking. He was flashing his wardrobe and jewelry, they were flashing wigs, make-up, fancy shoes, and skin, lots of skin; well it was the summertime!

Now, the shopping is over. Once back in the house, I asked my stepfather, "What was that about? Who were those people?" He very nonchalantly said, while laughing at me, that he was a pimp out of Cleveland and those were some of his women. They boost clothes for him. That day I learned a new word for stealing. As I recall that relationship and new way of shopping was short lived. I remember placing an order for a winter leather coat that never came, everything ended that fall.

While the exposure to that lifestyle didn't last very long, it was long enough for me to start thinking about a different way a man could make some money, pimping. At that time, during my youthful dumb thinking, it sounded like the perfect job. You get to drive nice cars, and you get to dress nice. I wasn't into all that flash, but I was into dressing; I liked nice clothes. You also get to surround yourself with women; that thought for me, simply meant endless sex. When you couple the fact that this was the era of "Playboy" magazine and teenage boys having a healthy appetite toward anything sex related, whether we were getting any or not, it seemed like an adventure worth considering.

Somewhere back in junior high school, I took part in a type of aptitude testing that was geared towards identifying jobs in your adult life you might be suited for. One of the jobs that showed up at the top of my list was Forest Ranger. Yea, it surprised me too, but for some reason it got stuck in my head, Forest Ranger Stringer. I never researched it but rather imagined working at different forests and National Parks. When I compared the ranger job, spending time in tree houses with a pair of binoculars, keeping an eye on things in the woods to Pimping, the choice seemed easy. I didn't think that I would ever have another thought about hanging out in the woods.

I never actually got the chance to talk to a pimp about the game. However, I did spend a couple of hours once, talking to someone that was close to that world. That was a two-hour reality check for me that made it perfectly clear that there was nothing about the way I was thinking that was pimp worthy. I later read a book titled "Iceberg Slim." It was about the life of a pimp and exposed the real pimp game. That book really confirmed my lack of pimp ability.

The person I had the conversation with was around these people because he was a drug dealer. I explained to him my rationale for why I thought that I could make pimping work for me. At that time, I hadn't read the book, but I knew some of the basic components. That limited knowledge told me that pimps treated women like shit. They would beat them and get some hooked on drugs to get them to do their bidding.

My approach was going to be just the opposite. I knew that I was a nice guy and could never pimp like that. My thoughts were that if pimps achieved that lifestyle by being cruel to women, how much more would they submit to a person that treated them not just nice, but very well. I was thinking more like a partnership relationship as opposed to what seemed to me to be a master/slave arrangement.

When I finished laying out my plan, the drug dealer laughed so loud and long, he developed a headache. He first declared that not only would that not work, but that my "dumb ass" would go from pimping to being pimped in a very short period of time. What he said next is the real reason I chose to put this foolishness here, in this chapter. He said, "When you control a person's mind, their ass will follow, the pimp game is mind control!"

He went on to explain that the cruelty part of the game leads to control of the mind. That control gives them the power to make demands, he said that my approach, being the nice guy, would only give me the power to make suggestions not demands. At that point, he told me that most pimps die young and broke and the women age fast and spend time in and out of jail.

He told me that my plan was more in-line with being a "Mac Man," short for Macaroni, that's someone that has women taking care of them. This is different than pimping because these are women with real jobs and spending their hard-earned money on these guys. He went on to say I was a decent looking guy and could probably GET to be a "Mac Man" one day. At that point, the only thing I wanted to GET was as far away from that conversation and that lifestyle as possible. Clearly, pimping and macking was not going to be in my future. Thank God! Now, the Forest Ranger option is back, but barely hanging on by a thin thread.

I warned you that this was going to be a ride on my "Foolish Train." However, that brief but impressionable time in my youth introduced me to some knowledge of the power of the mind and mind control; Not something most boys my age was thinking about. Now, back to what I really want to talk about, the slogan, "A mind is a terrible thing to waste." This was referring to the wasting of a person's mind by not affording them the opportunity to attend college. The ability to go to college is often controlled by factors beyond one's reach. The biggest one being financial, which is what the slogan was addressing. Of course, other things can come to bear that can make it difficult to attend school.

Truth is, there are many other ways to waste a person's mind. These can be things that we do have control over, things like what we watch on television and in movies, the music we listen to, the electronic games we play, and the social networks we surround ourselves with (friends, associates, and the crowds we hang around). The reason I'm talking about our minds in this chapter is because our minds are the most impactful part of who we are and what we can become. We have all heard people described as, "they are a strong leader" or perhaps, "he or she is a strong competent leader of something." Most of the time, people are not talking about the physicality of the leader, but rather their leadership skills; how their mind works.

Leaders come in all sizes, shapes, and genders, much like in golf. People who play the game of golf, no matter the level, but especially at the professional level, know that the biggest part of trying to master that game is mental. That is always a key component to becoming a successful leader. It's about how and what you think about, your processing ability, your mind.

"Fake it 'til you make it."

What do you think about when you hear that phrase? For most people, it paints a picture of someone that is phony, faking like they are something that they are not. I see something different, I see a type or form of self-motivation, of self-leadership. I see someone that has their eyes on a prize that they haven't been able to capture yet. This is my interpretation because I see a difference between a fake and someone striving for a better life or lifestyle.

During the summer break, between our grandson's junior and senior years at college, he flew down from Indiana to spend some time with his Ohio relatives. He stayed with us, so we got to spend some quality time together. Upon his visit's end, during the ride back to the airport, I asked him a question that had some relevance to leadership. I knew that he was offered a position at the beginning of his sophomore year, that is usually reserved for juniors and seniors. At the time of the offer, I questioned the wisdom in taking on a task like that so early in his college career. The position was to head an organization which came with a fair amount of coordination, meetings, and travel.

He accepted the position and did very well in moving the

organization forward. I asked him why he was so confident that he could lead that group, given his heavy workload at college. His answer surprised me. He said it was because of something I had said to him when I was sharing some of the basics at becoming a good pool shooter. We have a pool table in our great room, and he liked to play on it. On one of their family visits, while he was playing, I told him something that he is now about to repeat to me. He said that I once told him that when you're shooting pool, you can't just focus on the shot you are about to take without considering the next shot or perhaps the next two shots. He said that he never forgot that. At the time, I was only thinking pool, but his thoughts went much deeper. He applied the success of pool shooting to the overall tapestry of dealing with life's decisions.

He made it clear that he had become very good at looking forward. He had gotten comfortable with making decisions, but only after considering the possible long-term impacts. He understood that the results of any right now decision, could show up in the future, so that possibility needed to be factored into each decision, especially the big ones. Sometimes when I'm shooting, I think about that conversation. It doesn't seem to help my game, but it's a good memory.

We all deal with the right-now decisions on issues. However, good leaders, whether it's leading yourself or a group, need to always consider the future impact after you are on the other side of whatever decision you make in real time. How we think matters. The decisions we make play a major part in shaping who we are and ultimately the life and lifestyles we live. Bad decisions can have unfavorable consequences, while good ones are generally rewarded. These get to become byproducts of our minds and self-leadership actions.

Back in the 80s, I went to a professional basketball game at the Richfield Coliseum in Cleveland, Ohio. This was the home arena for the Cleveland Cavaliers. The game was between the Cavaliers and the Philadelphia 76ers. I don't remember a lot about the actual game that night. However, I do recall the play of Charles Barkley of the 76ers. He had a good game and was fun to watch. The thing I remember the most was coming home with a severe bruise on my right thigh.

Back then, there was a very popular activity at sporting events called "The Wave." It was something fun that everybody could take part in. It was simply standing with your hands raised then quickly sitting back down. It would start in one section and move around the arena in one direction thus creating the movement of a continuous up and down motion resembling a wave. At this point, most normal thinking people reading this are wondering why this event is in a chapter on leadership. I'll try to connect the dots.

I've spent the majority of this chapter focusing on the words "leadership and leader" and some associated activities and functions tied to those words. For me, when I really think about leadership, I see it as one part of a three-part choreographed movement. I see it as a three-legged stool. The end results of leadership are tied closely to the other two words, "Responsibility" and "Preparedness."

Back to the basketball game. The "wave" that night, started a few sections to the right of where I was sitting and was moving in the direction away from me. That meant that I had some time to think about whether or not I was going to participate. My first thought for some reason was, "No." However, by the time it got around to my section, I was an all-in, "Yes." Each section seemed to get louder and louder and now I wanted to represent my section. When it got to me, I was hyped and ready to show that I was having a good time. The second before I attempted to stand, was the end of my fun for the night. From that time on, I was in pain and ready to go home!

Lost in all the excitement was the fact that my right leg was under the arm of my seat and extended out from the seat. When I jumped up, that arm pulled me back down with a punctuated pain I can still recall to this day. Here's how those three words have bearing on the memory of that Cleveland event. I am the "leader" of myself and "responsible" for the well-being of my body. However, I saw something I wanted to do but didn't "prepare" myself properly for it. My right leg was not in the right position to do what I wanted to accomplish.

Sure, doing the "Wave" was not a big life changing decision/activity. However, some decisions could be more like a "Tidal Wave" with potentially major implications and those three words will still have bearing. Those three demand our full attention because they will always be in-play whenever "leading" is in-play.

This was one of the last chapters I wrote because it took me a long time to really wrap my head around how complex the topic of leadership can be. There is no "Leadership 101" that's a fit for all situations. It's too dynamic. It has many intertwining components that can impact, not just projects within organizations, but life itself.

Leadership is something none of us can escape. The real questions are how do we see ourselves within it, how well do we perform within it, and do we learn from our mistakes. Understanding your position in life, that you really are a leader, is a solid foundation to build on, and to help deal with this wonderful and sometimes crazy thing we call living life.

CHAPTER 9

-THE FINALS; THOUGHTS, A THANK YOU, A QUESTION, A PRAYER

With every beginning, there's a middle and ending.
Live your best "DASH;" it's the only one you've got!

"Life is not a dress rehearsal and time is not a renewable re-source." I wish that I had come up with that phrase because it's true and it would have made me look intuitive. That one got by me, but the following is some of my closing thoughts on the subject.

"Life" is the most competitive race any of us will ever run. It represents some of our most penal, saddest, joyous, unforgiving, uplifting, rewarding, hate driven, and loving experiences that drives the emotions that helps to shape us as human beings.

Life, we're born into it; no control. We're born into some ethnic group/culture; no control. We all at some point find ourselves in some social-economic echelon; some control. We all need to look in the mirror periodically and give an honest assessment of the person looking back at us, total control.

When my first wife was in the hospital dying, a minister friend came to check on her one evening. At her bedside, he told me something about life and death that wasn't new but the way he phrased it has stayed with me. He said, "This is a race we are all running, some run it faster than others."

What he said was a true statement. How long our race and how it might end are mostly things we have little control over. However, how we RUN our race is something we can control and modify.

This world that we have been thrust into at birth is a wonderment of many facets, it's like a maze of many intersecting options. Each choice and path carrying its own set of risks and rewards, the longer we walk the paths and make choices, good and bad, the clearer our path forward should become for future intersecting/ transitional decisions.

Living life has taught me many things. I say "taught me" because we all go through things, but we don't always learn from them. One of the most impactful lessons for me has been understanding the power of decision making and how fast it can change the course of our lives.

Our lives are lived in moments, one after another. That

means the situations we face and the decisions we make also happen in moments. Once a moment in time passes, it is gone. We are all familiar with the term "do over." Something happens, and someone suggests a "do over." Another chance to advance a different result to some occurrence.

However, what is being suggested does not exist. The "do over" is impossible because what happened, happened in a moment that has passed. The so call "do over" is actually a second chance to try to get something right; to fix a wrong; to change an outcome that previously happened. Truth is, you may or may not get a second chance. First time decisions and actions might be our only chance to deal with a certain situation. When those times present themselves, we need to make the best decisions and take the best course of action we possibly can.

One of my goals in writing this book was to highlight this game of life we all have been forced to play and the seriousness of the role each one of us is either playing or will play. Also, the importance of learning the rules that are in play in each phase of our lives as we move forward. Another focus was to drive the point that the decisions we make each day carries the possibility of having a major impact on our futures.

It's been said, "You can't be who you are, until you know who you are."

Let that statement sink in for a while then ask yourself, Who am I, really? How do I label myself? How do I prioritize the things that impact my life?

Life is never static; it's always moving and changing. When you are part of something that has the ability and the propensity at some point to transform your life, you need to have a good understanding as to who you are and what your goals are. The longer it takes to figure those two things out, the more problematic and confusing a person's life can become. Unfortunately, some people live their entire life at the whims of what society and other people say how they should think and what they should do. This could happen for a variety of reasons. They might have never quite figured out who they are or how they fit in. Perhaps they know exactly who they are but might not have the courage to be true to themselves. The possibility of never having solid goals could also be a factor.

Most people find it difficult to go against the norms of society. Life does seem to flow better when you are swimming with the current of popular opinion rather than against it. Truth is, this is how most people think and act. That's why most people fall into the category of average. For the most part, average is easier; average is comfortable. You don' find many average people becoming millionaires but you also don't see many incarcerated either. You can live a very good lifestyle within the boundaries of going along with the flow and following the rules. The key to being content there or in any other category still lies within knowing who you are and what your goals are.

I believe that most people start off as dreamers. Not dreams of driving used cars and living a lower, middle-class lifestyle but rather big dreams, lavish and over the top dreams. Dreams that will make their family proud and everyone else envious of their accomplishments and lifestyle. The reason we dream like that is because we know that it's possible; we see it all around us. We watch T.V., go to the movies, and see the endless options of what possibly can happen to us, so we dream on.

Young adults are seldom content when they are dreaming about their future lives. However, the closer they get to embracing their reality, the closer they are to transitioning to contentment. They are hardly ever content when chasing something they really want. In most cases, contentment, if it wasn't your original dream, is a type of settling or embracing something that is different from that dream. It's like a "catch 22," We've always heard "chase your dreams," which means you never settle for anything less.

When dreams fall short, there is a "thin line" between accepting reality and embracing it. When you embrace it, you start to move your mental state in a positive direction. When you just accept it, you can start to slip into a mental state of depression. Somewhere along the path of our life's journeys, there will be times when we will need to reconcile between dreams/ambitions and reality. That reconciliation is the first step toward contentment.

This is a typical scenario that lands most of us in the average/middle-class category. Over time, through circumstances of living life, your current lifestyle starts to shape the dream that once was. Reality is setting in and the dream is getting smaller. You are drifting fast and hard toward average. At some point, average gets to be your realistic goal. You start to tell yourself that average is good because you have been sliding so far away from your initial dreams, you are happy to be able to stop at average. At average, you assess where you are and get content. You can plainly see those doing better and those not doing as well as you and you are thankful that you're not in the latter group.

No matter who you are or what your station in life is, there will always be people doing better and worse than you. Each person has to put their own values on doing better and worse. Contentment can come at any level once you mentally embrace your situation. I believe the closer you are to being content, the closer you are to being happy. That contentment gets to be a byproduct of wisdom and wisdom a byproduct to adjustments of sound decisions and good judgment over time. Everyone wants to experience their own version of happiness.

I also believe that some of life's counterbalances help keep the scale of happiness even, and us sane, are laughter, fun, healthy relationships, and religious faith. Another is finding and hanging on to the things you enjoy doing. I call them things you do for you. These can prove to be welcome stop gaps / pressure relief valves within life's daily grind. My list includes listening to music, shooting pool, playing golf, and the card game Pinochle. I also like looking at the different cloud formations, it's like mini vacations for my brain. I find some to be quite extraordinary.

I was passing through our bedroom one day and my wife was watching "The Steve Harvey Show." I typically don't watch game or talk shows but what Mr. Harvey was saying got my attention. He was giving some advice to a woman in his audience that wanted help concerning her husband's job position. He was a substitute teacher for ten years and wanted to be a full-time teacher. I thought his response to her was on point. He told her that her husband's dream was not big enough. In short, he said, if you dream about being a full-time teacher and fall short, substitute teaching is where you could land; but if you set your sites on being a principal and fall short, you might end up being a full-time teacher.

What he said next has application for all of us, he said when we are dreaming about what life could be for us, our problem gets to be not that we aim too high and miss it as much as it is aiming low and hitting it. He went on to say that when we dream big, we invite God into the situation because we serve a "Big God." What he said was profound and I was in agreement with him.

One of my challenges in writing this book was to steer away from religion. It was difficult because I love and serve my Lord and Savior Jesus Christ. Truth is that every point I tried to make could have been referenced back to something in the Bible. I'm not ashamed of my religious beliefs and those that know me know that to be true. I simply wanted to present some life issues that we all are dealing with and not have to debate the religious or political sides of those topics. I also made an effort to steer clear of politics. Avoiding the pull of those two dynamics wasn't always easy. In fact, to express and define my position on certain issues proved to be nearly impossible, but I tried.

Over my lifetime, I've seen many advancements and setbacks throughout society. Pick any subject, category, topic or thing and that statement would hold true for me and any other senior person. That witnessing of roller coaster good and bad also holds true for most people, not just seniors. The question that I keep coming back to is how are we as Black people advancing? How are we running our "mile?" Most of our setbacks are newsworthy and thankfully now, show up on the news medias. Knowledge of the problems are important but what about the other stuff, the advancements, or the lack thereof.

There are a lot of statistics available about the advancement and contributions that we as a people and culture have made to society. However, the "mile race" question is answered more personally than statistically. It's like in politics, good or bad political decisions are personally measured at the local level. How did that decision/direction impact me? Likewise, the direction we see and feel the Black culture is moving toward is also viewed from a personal perspective.

For many years, even with the obvious setbacks, I could see us making forward progress in many areas. However, most of the time, it seemed like we were still running the wrong race. We were just getting better at running it; the "mile run." Now, I believe that we as a people, are finally running the right race, the "mile relay" and passing our batons forward. While I believe that to be true, we are still not winning enough races. We still need a lot of help to catch up, but we are starting to help each other more. I'm encouraged by some of our positive, cultural changing tides. I'm also optimistic that this book might be seen as a positive add to that forward movement.

I want to offer a sincere "Thank You" for taking the time to consider my thoughts and words. I'm hopeful there was something worthy of your time within these pages.

How we think has an influence on how we see. When we have negative thoughts, we tend to see the bad or dark side of whatever situation we might find ourselves in and promotes "small thinking." The flip side of that is looking for the good or positive in things as we deal with life issues/opportunities and opens us up to think "large."

I heard a story once about a shoe manufacturer sending two of his salesmen to a tropical island to prospect for sales opportunities. Their returning reports could not have been more different. One reported that the majority of the people didn't wear shoes, it would be a waste of time and resources. The other reported that the majority of the people didn't wear shoes, unlimited opportunity for sales! They saw the same things, but their thoughts were different. How you think is how you see.

Are you a glass half empty or half full person? The glass half empty people strive to be schoolteachers. The half full people set their sights on being school principals.

My constant "Question" to everyone and to me is, "are we dreaming/thinking big enough?"

One of my favorite verses in the Bible is Jeremiah 29:11, "For I know the plans I have for you declares the Lord, plans to prosper you and not harm you, plans to give you hope and a future." (NIV) This verse helps me to focus on the "positive" when confronting life and to strive towards being a glass half full person.

My "Prayer" is for each of us to run our life's race with enthusiasm, hopefulness, and purpose that will result in a great life to pass forward. Why? Because there are people counting on us; that's reason enough!